FAMILY SYSTEMS AND BEYOND

FAMILY SYSTEMS AND BEYOND

**Jason Montgomery, Ph.D. and
Willard Fewer, M.Sc.**

University of Alberta, Edmonton, Canada

HUMAN SCIENCES PRESS, INC.
72 FIFTH AVENUE
NEW YORK, N.Y. 10011-8004

To Barbara and Roxanne

Copyright © 1988 by Human Sciences Press, Inc.
72 Fifth Avenue, New York, New York 10011

Printed in the United States of America
987654321

Library of Congress Cataloging in Publication Data

Montgomery, Jason.
  Family systems and beyond.

  Bibliography: p.
  Includes index.
  1. Family. 2. System theory. 3. System analysis.
I. Fewer, Willard. II. Title. [DNLM: 1. Family.
HQ 728 M787f]
HQ728.M5725 1988   306.8'5   87-3816
ISBN 0-89885-386-9

CONTENTS

5

ACKNOWLEDGMENTS

Many people have contributed to this book and acknowledging their input is not only fair but, also, it is a partial payment on a debt so great that it can never be repaid.

We appreciate the hundreds of students over the past few years who have suffered the slings and arrows of partially developed ideas and who have asked the difficult questions that kept us thinking and revising this book. More specifically, we appreciate the Family Studies Graduate Students here at the University of Alberta who have discussed these ideas with us and whose contributions have indicated both the value of what we were trying to do and the places where we could do better.

Even more specifically, we wish to thank Judy Ballantyne for her careful reading of an early draft and her comments on style, and Karen Argento for her patience and skill in making the countless revisions and the trivial changes.

PREFACE

This monograph has been written for use by students of the family. "Students" refers to people who are interested in understanding family interaction, who have had some course work (or have done independent study) in the family, and who are interested in inquiring further into the mysteries of family process.

In writing the book, we attempted to accomplish four goals, three of which were theoretical. The theoretical goals are as follows. First, the book is an attempt to help students to understand families from a particular approach, that which is called systems theory. The book provides information about the systems approach and it contains a glossary of systems terms.

Students are introduced to the systems way of viewing families. The systems view has developed over many years and there is a well developed systems perspective, a set of terms, and a body of literature and research which uses these terms. In this book, presently used systems terms are discussed and defined and we trust that the discussion and the resulting glossary will assist students in understanding systems-based literature.

There are, of course, other ways to consider families, but the systems approach is one that is frequently used by family specialists and, equally important, students have found this approach to be a useful way to think about families. The book attempts to bring together various systems ideas and to present these ideas as a unified whole.

Secondly, the book attempts to transcend the systems approach. In this case, transcending means revising and adding to. The existence of some terminological ambiguity suggests that some presently used systems terms need to be revised or even eliminated; such changes are incorporated in the glossary and a rationale for the revisions is presented.

The systems perspective is a contemporary and very lively framework and it is steadily growing and developing; new ideas are being added to it and changes are being made. This book attempts to further the development of the theory by augmenting it with ideas which will make the theory more applicable to families and which will allow for a more thorough analysis of family processes.

Our third goal associated with theory was to illustrate the way that a self-correcting theory could be developed and used. The development of the glossary and the theoretical model follows a logic: First, a set of criteria is established and presented and these criteria are used to determine the value of subsequently used terms and ideas. Secondly, terms are defined in keeping with the criteria and then the terms are used to discuss families. The terms are used both separately and in conjunction with other terms. The use of each term, both singularly and in conjunction with other terms is dictated by the previously established criteria. And last, the terms are explicitly presented in the glossary and in the model which completes the book.

This method of theory construction can be self-correcting in that the value of terms and their fit can be monitored by comparing the use of the term with the preceding criteria. If there is incongruence between the term and the criteria, either the criteria or the term's definition can be revised.

We believe this process worked well for us. We had goals (enhanced understanding of family systems; the creation of an integrated glossary) and the process allowed us to move toward our goals and to monitor our progress as we went along.

In addition to theoretically based goals, we had a more important goal: to help readers better understand family life and thereby improve their intimate relationships. In fact, theory is a means to that end; theory being only intellectual play unless it is applied to real situations and helps people to understand their lives, the lives of others, and the networks formed by these intersecting lives.

Using a theory to better understand family life and thereby improve this life seems like a reasonable goal, but understanding and improving require that we make an accurate analysis. It is unfortunate that accuracy is hard to achieve. The sources of inaccuracy will be considered in the next few paragraphs and then we will explain why, despite the likelihood of inaccuracy, we are going to present the theory and encourage application. We will also indicate what can be done to foster accuracy.

The analysis of family interaction involves applying one's ideas about families (one's theory) to some real-life family situation. The ideas can be either simplistic or sophisticated; they can be part of either a formal theory or an informal one. In any instance of analysis, some situation is "interpreted" or "understood" by explaining events in terms of theory. Theory always precedes analysis.

Theory not only precedes analysis, theory also focuses our attention on specific parts of family interaction and leads us to ignore other aspects of family life. For example, if we are interested in the way that sibling interaction reflects spousal interaction, we would probably neither see nor consider the family's way of adapting to change or the transactions of the parents with their families of orientation.

Analysis is not only partial, it is frequently inaccurate. Inaccuracy can have its source in either (or both) the theory or the application. Theory may lead to inaccuracy because of the theory's incompleteness. For example, a theory that contains the idea that a family is only a collection of individuals cannot be used to analyze accurately the effect of the family's emotional intensity on interaction nor can it be used to understand conflict or harmony or other group processes.

Application of theory may also produce inaccuracy because we apply theory to that which we see and hear and otherwise sense. Our perceptions are affected by our biases—we see what we expect is there. We have biases about how families "should" behave because we experienced a particular family form in growing up and we "know" what works and what does not work in families. These biases distort our perception and we fail to see what is not congruent with our preconceptions.

Inasmuch as most of our "knowledge" about "proper" family behavior has been implicitly taught through family experiences, we are not even aware of our biases. Biases exist at unconscious and seldom considered levels of thought, and because they are deeply embedded and hidden we do not know when they intrude and affect our analysis nor do we know when they becloud our perception.

Analyzing family systems of which we are a part is likely to be even more inaccurate than our analysis of others' relationships. Not only do we have the same problem of bias, we have an additional problem in that we are likely to analyze our relationships in such a way that we feel good about ourselves. Inasmuch as our analysis of our own families will emphasize that which supports our self-image, we can never be sure whether any such analysis is an attempt to find out "what is happening" or is an attempt to justify our behavior to ourselves and/or others.

The second problem with family analysis is that the application of theory to interaction involves rationality and much of family-related behavior is not rational. Applying a rational theory to irrational behavior is similar to measuring some quantity of air in units of linear feet or in centimeters; that is, an inappropriate standard is being used. Since most of our family-related behavior is not rational, applying a reason-based theory will not work; the theory is inappropriate to the behavior to which it is applied.

So, our problem can be stated as follows: We want to make the theory useful but it seems as though this usefulness will be elusive. Put another way, our goal is to help students better understand their own lives, their family relationships, and the family relationships of others. On the other hand, our experience indicates that the achievement of this understanding requires that we eliminate biases that we do not even know we have, that we reduce the self-serving nature of our analysis, and that we rationally consider irrational behavior. This, as they say, is a tall order.

There are some ways in which we can reduce the problems that attend analysis. These approaches can help us analyze more ably and can help us improve our relationships.

First, we should be aware that we are biased. Knowledge of biases is not sufficient to eliminate their effect, but there can be no bias reduction without this first step of awareness. Other steps in the process of removing bias include introspection, the awareness of feelings, the explicit consideration of structure and process in one's family of orientation, and the feelings that we have regarding this structure and process, and the direct facing of one's ideas regarding what is "healthy" and what is "wrong" in families.

The second way that we can improve our relationship life through analysis is by sharing our analysis with the family members who are being analyzed. This is especially true and especially important if we are analyzing our own family. If we share our perceptions, and engage in the discussion which "share" implies, we will get the other's independently derived opinion about what is happening. Even if the second opinion is inaccurate (it will probably not be any more inaccurate than ours), it can help us increase the accuracy of our analysis in that it will put our view in question and we will have to reconsider the ideas that seemed so "correct" to us.

Sharing is also important in that it minimizes the deleterious effects of analysis. Analysis tends to separate people in a relationship: this separation happens because analysis requires that we objectify the other and that we see the other's behavior as distinct and independent from our own. (Later, we call this "punctuation.") When we analyze, we tend to see ourselves as the unfortunate soul, the one who gets the dirt, and we overlook our own contribution to the situation. Even though the lives of family members are intertwined, analysis provides a false sense of independence; sharing reminds us that "we are all in this together."

If you must analyze, at least share with your mate the fruits of your analysis and get that other person's view. Sharing of the thoughts can bring people together; more specifically, the sharing of relationship ideas can bring people even closer.

The third way to improve relationships by better understanding them concerns rationality and feelings. Let us acknowledge that feelings do direct both our family-related behavior and our observation of family-related behavior and accept that to be a fact of life. Having acknowledged irrational elements, let us consider the importance of rationality. (Clearly, we the authors must view the rational consideration of family life as important or there would exist no reason to write a book on systems theory as it applies to family life. Nor would there be any reason to read it.)

The rational consideration of family life will occur because we are humans and humans can never leave anything alone. We are curious; we want to know how things work. Human beings could no more avoid attempting to understand families than attempting to inquire into DNA, or the stars, or into all that exists between.

Also, we humans will inquire into families because we think that such inquiry and the resulting knowledge makes our lives better. The evidence indicating that the social part of our lives is worse than it was 2500 years ago is approximately equal to the evidence that this same part of our lives is better. Nevertheless, it is an important part of the contemporary worldview that knowledge and the mastery of the earth makes for better lives. With some reservations, we hold that view and we agree that knowledge is better than ignorance and that understanding can make for richer lives. This belief is the foundation of the book; it served as its raison d'etre.

So, whether we want to do it or not, we humans will study families. Inasmuch as that is the case, let us study families in the best way we can, using the most complete theory we have, making its terms clear and unambiguous, broadening the theory so that it includes family life, and talking about theory as being in a state of development. Let us work to develop a mental toughness that will allow us to consider our biases, how these biases becloud our perception, and, having done this, observe and inquire into families and attempt to find out what it is that moves people in a family to interact the way they do.

In the preceding paragraph two ideas are expressed. The first of these is that the book should help us to clarify our language, sharpen our thinking and thereby improve our analysis. The second is that we should actually use the theory and analyze family life. The exploration of these two ideas is the goal of this book.

First we will present ideas about families as systems. Secondly, as we present ideas, we will use a dramatic presentation about a particular family as a source of examples. We will analyze the Spencers, a fictional family, whose interaction processes are expressed in such a way that they reflect a family systems perspective.

Using a fictional family has many advantages. The members do not care if they are analyzed. In fact, families of fiction exist to be analyzed; they are created for that reason. The characters have no feelings to hurt so we do not have to protect them from either the glare of public attention or the cruelty of our analysis. We do not have to change their names or disguise their identities.

We are experienced in the analysis of fictional families. Thoughtful theatergoers have been analyzing families for thousands of years and we have come to know families of drama (and television and film) very well. These families have been objectified, analyzed, and discussed. Virtually everyone knows about Hamlet's folks, J.R.'s family problems, and Oedipus's difficulties both in honoring his mother and in being a dutiful husband.

Families of fiction take on a reality equal to that of real families. Fictional and nonfictional families have many similarities. Both are the result of the urge to create. Both exist in persons' minds. Behavior in both follows a particular script, a script that means something to family members. Both are illusory and consist of remembered fragments of shared experiences.

Family drama that lasts, that stands the test of time, entertains and, more important, informs us about family processes. It does so because it taps the essence of family life: the benefits and costs of our attempts to share our private and intimate lives with others over time. We know when drama *works* because the persons are believable: their situations, no matter how bizarre, somehow make sense. In families that are well presented, the language fits the characters being portrayed, it fits the way the persons interact, and it fits the situation which provides the context. Dramatic presentations that *work* get to the essence of family life; there is little padding, little which is superfluous.

These, then, are our goals, some of the problems associated with writing the book and using the ideas, ways to limit these difficulties, and the reasons we have used drama for analysis and exemplification in meeting the goals we set ourselves.

Chapter 1

INTRODUCTION

THE DEVELOPMENT OF THE SYSTEMS VIEW

The major goal of social science is to explain why people act the way they do. Social scientists have attempted to answer these questions: What are the factors that influence behavior? How do the person's mental processes interact with externally sourced influences so that particular kinds of behavior result? Many answers had their day and were eventually found to lack clarity, consistency, universality, or good sense. Answers once in favor were discarded, only to be replaced by others which in turn were themselves replaced.

In the beginning there was "cause," and explanations of human behavior sought this cause. Some thought that original sin was the cause, others believed in instincts. The "will to power" had its true believers as did the profit motive, race, and gender. Each of these causes was thought to be the basis of human behavior.

The idea of a single cause of human behavior hardly survived the nineteenth century in learned circles. The search for a single cause was replaced by a search for many causes and a concern for the relative power of these causes. This search continues to the present day and has been advanced by sophisticated analytical techniques such as path analysis and by the complex statistical massaging of data afforded by computer-based analysis.

Parallel to the growth of the idea of multicausation was the emergence of the systems view. Some observers and theoreticians replaced multicausation with mutual causation since the idea of linear causality, even multifactor linear causality, was incongruous with their view of the behavior of persons and groups of persons. Systems theorists drew from the emerging science of cybernetics and from game theory, and they began to see human behavior in terms of the exchange and handling of information, the context in which the behavior occurred, and the mutual involvement of the actors.

People using a systems framework were interested in answering different questions than those of the searchers after cause. Questions for systems-based analysis included: "What elements of a social system contemporaneously affect and are affected by other elements of the social system and what is the nature of this mutual effect?" And later, there were more difficult questions: "How does the behavior of different system components fit together? How does the fit come about? How does the components' fit affect the functioning of the system as a whole? How does the fit affect the functioning of the components?"

The questions were and still are theoretically important and former views of interaction failed to answer them adequately. The importance of context, the mutuality of interaction, the interpenetration of one system with another are elements of individual and group behavior that cannot be addressed in a cause-based analysis. Yet, our experience indicates that these ideas are essential to understanding family life and that theories that fail to address such phenomena are incomplete and need either replacement or reformulation. Systems theory, because it addressed these important matters, emerged and became accepted.

The systems view has helped us to understand family life. We have learned about the ways families work and about the interactive and reciprocal nature of family behavior. New therapeutic approaches based on the family as a system have been effective, and therapeutic techniques have become more sophisticated. The systems approach has helped us to understand the richness of family life.

The systems view is comprehensive since it includes society, family, parts of families, persons, and the relationships between elements at all levels. It can be broadened to include such diverse perspectives as symbolic interaction, the developmental approach, and exchange theory. There is a place in systems theory for Olson's "circumplex" model (Olson, Sprenkle, & Russell, 1979), the ABCX model as stated by Hill (1958) and in its more recent forms (McCubbin & Patterson, 1983).

At the same time, not surprisingly, there have been some difficulties with the systems view. For example, consider the "cause" of behavior. In systems theory, there *is* no cause, since behavior is interactional and processual and has no discernible beginning. (There will be more on this later.) Nevertheless, the idea of "cause" has persisted. Even though "mutual cause" (Frank's behavior was caused by Bill and, simultaneously, Bill reacted to what Frank did) replaced a single cause, the idea of cause has maintained its importance as a way of explaining behavior and interaction.[1]

There are other problems, too. An important part of systems analysis is that systems are composed of levels and the properties that attend components at any particular level are different from the properties of components at other levels and different from the properties of the whole.[2] An automobile, for example, has different properties than has any one of its components (wheel, gasoline, engine, etc.) Although this principle applies to families as well as automobiles, systems theorists have disregarded it and they have given to elements at one level characteristics that belong to some other part of the family system. The idea of the "family mind" is just one example of this confusion. Mind, the property of a person, was bestowed on the family and then, to make matters worse, "family mind" was ordained a "cause" (Reiss & Oliveri, 1983).[3]

Complicating inquiry into cause was (and is) the persistent notion expounded by humanists and phenomenologists that the source of human behavior is to be found internally and that persons generate their own behavior from the stuff of their dreams and imaginings and thought. Systems theory has not dealt well with mental constructs and even the consideration of "information," the closest that systems theory comes to mental processes, has stressed the mechanistic rather than the creative elements of perception, thought, and communication.

Obviously, an explanation of human behavior continues to elude us and we do not yet know why we humans act the way we do. It is true that we now are able to justify our behavior and impugn the motives of others, but these activities are only rationalizations and not explanations. Tell me why we act intimately at home and unpleasantly at work or why we behave benignly when we are away from home yet act violently toward fellow family members. Why can't we get others to do what we want them to do? Why do we resist change, even change that we know to be in our best interests? Why do people change their behavior when we wish they would stay as they are? What is the source of intimacy?

But this book is not about behavior in general, it is about action and interaction in families. The questions addressed include: What holds a family together? What are the forces that drive people apart to even such a degree that a onetime intimate becomes an enemy? What promotes adaptability? Why can some families adapt and remain integrated while other families are not able to adapt? Why do other families adapt but then fall apart? What is the relationship between a family and elements of the larger social setting? What do families do with information? How does a family's consensus and the concerted activity based on that consensus come about?

Questions of this type are the subject of this book and we will attempt to answer them by developing, clarifying, and transcending the family systems paradigm. Despite our belief that systems analysis provides the best way of explaining family-centered behavior, we believe that answers based on systems theory could be clarified, broadened, and connected with insights from other theories. We will try to find the answers as we sharpen the use and understanding of words and concepts, the tools of our trade. Sharper tools may lead to a sharper understanding of family life.

We have used ideas from systems theory to help us clarify systems theory. Systems theorists have followed principles as they developed the theory but, unfortunately, the principles, more often than not, have been implicit. We have made these principles explicit, applied them to systems terms, and clarified the terms on the basis of the principles. In other words, systems analysis has made two contributions to inquiry into families. First, it has provided insights into family processes; secondly, it has provided principles that can be applied to concepts and can thereby clarify them. We have used both of these contributions.

These two contributions of systems theory provide the basis for the major sections of the book. The remainder of this first chapter contains a statement of the principles that have guided our inquiry. We have given special consideration to the idea of cause. In the remainder of the book these principles will be used to establish a consistent and understandable view of the family as a system.[4]

THE PRINCIPLES

The following are the rules which have guided this inquiry into family systems.[5]

1. *Define the system being considered.*

Clarity is advanced by the careful specification of the system being considered. Although all mindful systems have common properties, no two systems are exactly the same and clarity demands that the system under consideration be explicitly specified.

A family and a person are each a type of system and general systems theory can be applied to each. However, as will be seen, a family has different characteristics than has a person, and it is an error, from the systems perspective, to confuse the properties of families and the characteristics of persons. The likelihood of making this error is reduced if the observer-analyst indicates explicitly the system being considered.

2. *Use appropriate language.*

Use language that refers to living systems, not language borrowed from the physical sciences (Dell, 1985). Avoid terms such as "power," "tension," "energy," "stress," "forces" (Bateson, 1979, p. 240) except as these terms refer to the physical (material) characteristics of the parts of the system (Bogdan, 1984).[6]

When mindful systems are being considered, not only is inappropriate language to be avoided, but also thinking associated with physical systems. For example, "environmentalism" (. . . "the environment acts as a kind of cause upon the behavior of organisms" (Bogdan, 1984, p. 381)) and other deterministic explanations are to be avoided. A theory of behavior should have a place for volition.

As opposed to physical systems, systems (such as individuals) with a mind, or systems (such as families) with minded components, never simply react; they creatively interact with their environment.[7] In minded systems, sensations of reality are managed and this managed information is the basis of its subsequent activity.

It is commonly held that some event in the system's context is the source (or even the "cause") of the system's response. We disagree with this commonly held idea and our disagreement is based on our understanding of perception and on our experience. Studies of perception indicate that an organism never responds to an event in a direct way; it responds to *its own interpretation* of the event. Moreover, there need be no actual event in order for the organism to act, for an organism *can create its own "event,"* one that is born of its own imaginings, hopes, and fears, and the contrived "event" may have little or no basis in reality.

When we consider our experience, we get the clear impression that perception and thought provide the impetus for action. Inasmuch as these abilities exist in the system prior to the occasion of the external event, the system's "response" then uses preexisting energy, preexisting perceptual capacities, preexisting information management capabilities, preexisting experience, and preexisting decision-making processes. To see behavior in some stimulus-response paradigm is to miss the point that these internal elements predate the external event, that they affect the way that the news of the event is handled, and that they substantially affect the system's response.

Inasmuch as physical systems differ from living systems in essential ways, the understanding of both types of systems is advanced if terms are used that are specific to each system type. Using terms specific to each type of system has several advantages. It helps to differentiate between the two types of systems, it helps us to appreciate the unique properties of minded systems, and it helps us to better understand personal behavior and family interaction.

It should be noted that living systems have components that are subject to physical laws and the application of physical science terms to these nonmindful components is appropriate. When we stub our toe, the pain we feel is the result of the physical properties of the rock and the physical properties of our foot. We wear seat belts to safeguard ourselves by minimizing the chance of our becoming a projectile. And we age.

3. *Avoid nonexplanations.*

A nonexplanation is one in which some undefined concept (such as "natural progression") is substituted for careful analysis. The nonexplanation then parades as an explanation and is doubly damaging because it does not explain what it purports to explain and, because it hides the fact of our ignorance, disinclines us from searching further.

"Vitalistic" explanations are a case in point. A nonexplanation such as "in living interactional systems, order spontaneously arises" (Dell, 1982, p. 36) does not explain much, for we still have no explanation of the way that systems work; we only are told that such is their *nature.* In this case, the existence of order is acknowledged, but the *source* of order or the *function* that it serves remains unexplained. Such "explanations" do not increase understanding.

4. *Think of systems as unified entities.*

By definition, a system's parts are interconnected, but when a system's parts are separated and seen as acting independently, the system as a system is destroyed. Analysis that disjoins a system's components and thereby disfigures the interdependency of these components is not "systems analysis." It may be a thoughtful and valuable analysis but a systems analysis it is not.

When analysts split the system into components and then treat the parts as though they were separate, they create a "dualism." Dualisms hinder the understanding of family systems. One such dualism is: "The child's behavior stabilized the family." This statement leads to misunderstanding because one system element, the child's behavior, is separated from another element, the family's stability (Dell, 1982). Systems analysis maintains that the child's behavior and the family's stability cannot be separated for the reason that both the child's behavior and the family's stability are family system elements and they are thereby interconnected and interactive.

5. *Maintain strict differentiation of levels.*

Components of systems have different properties than have the whole systems of which they are a part. A family and a person are at different levels of the system and each has characteristics that are specifically theirs. Communication is a group property since it requires two people to negotiate the meaning of something; thinking, on the other hand, is the property of a person, because a family has no brain. A person can think but cannot communicate without another person; a group can communicate but can only communicate about that which has been thought by a group member.

To say that a problem or some other matter is "in the family" is to leave undefined its specific place in the family. That is, "in the family" fails to specify whether the problem or other matter exists at the family level or at the person level. For example, we can accurately say that interaction is "in the family" and we can say with equal accuracy that a member's headache is "in the family." Surely, though, a headache and an interaction sequence are not at the same family level and their being at different levels means that they require different treatment. "In the family," applied to elements at different levels, encourages the view that phenomena at different levels are to be treated the same. The term eliminates the necessity for a theorist to be precise.

It might be helpful to indicate some other terms that are appropriate to specific system levels. The following terms apply to persons; these properties are found "in," but not "of" or "by" families.

mind
ideas
shame
joy
expectations
perception
identification

The following terms apply to the properties and activities of *families:*

consensus
working agreement
interaction
harmony
conflict
hierarchy
communication

Klein and Hill (1979) appropriately used "by the family" to refer to an activity at the system level and "in the family" to refer to activity at the subsystem level. We believe this to be helpful.

We believe in the importance of keeping properties specific to system levels. Our experience teaches that success in so doing is not easy.

6. *Explaining systemic behavior requires care in that the system's unity must be preserved and the properties of the different levels must be acknowledged.*

This principle combines the previous two ideas and applies them to explanation. To be unambiguous, an explanation of a system's processes must recognize the system's unity and it must appreciate that different system levels have unique properties. For example, an expression such as "a mentally disturbed child is created by a sick family," is difficult to understand for two reasons.

In the first place, the sentence is equivocal for the reason that one of the properties of an individual (being sick) is given to a collectivity. A family may have interaction patterns that do not work—that is, the patterns do not accomplish what they were intended to accomplish—but a *family* cannot be "sick."

> The concept of family pathology is therefore, we believe, a confused one. It extends the unintelligibility of individual behavior to the unintelligibility of the group. . . .
> This instance of the transference of concepts derived from clinical biology into the realm of multiplicities of human beings is, in our view, unfruitful. (Laing & Esterson, 1964, p. 23)

In the same sense, a *family* cannot be "suicidal," "alcoholic," or "diabetic."

Secondly, the expression destroys the family's essential unity by indicating that the child, as a creation of the family, is somehow separate from the rest of the family. To differentiate a family member from the family is to liken a family to a production line and to make the member analogous to some product. However, the analogy is incorrect for, unlike the product of an assembly line which passively receives what comes its way and then is shipped off as a completed product, a family member is an active and interdependent agent who is always and forever tied to the family. Holding the idea that a family is a system and, as such, a unified entity, precludes the notion that some part can be created by the remainder.

It is, of course, possible and sometimes appropriate to indicate that a parent affects a child's mental health. This fits with systems analysis for the reason that the child and the parent are at the same logical level. There is no confusion of system levels because, unlike the categories "child" and "family," neither "parent" nor "child" is a category which includes the other as a member.

    7. *Avoid reification.*

As Miller (1984) defines it, "reification refers to the practice of labeling a behavioral pattern and then using the label as an explanation of the pattern" (p. 390). As an example, consider the term "mid-life crisis." This expression refers to a time in a person's life and some difficulties that frequently occur about that time. It is unfortunate that the term also is used as an explanation ("Oh well, he is just having a hard time with his mid-life crisis and that is why he is acting the way he is"). It is the use of this term as an explanation of behavior which is reification.

Such reification can be avoided if we make the same distinction between the word and what it represents that we make between a menu and the food we order and a map and the territory it represents. We would never think of eating the menu and have it taste like a soufflé nor would we expect our finger to get wet if we placed it on "Lake Superior" on a map. We have no difficulty with distinguishing the thing from its representation in these two areas, yet we seem to have great difficulty in differentiating our descriptions of behavior ("resistance," "mental illness," "enmeshment," "schizophrenic," "devitalized") from the action or interaction to which the words point.

When we confuse things with their symbols, we are led to believe that a person can actually be a schizophrenic or a family can be enmeshed. Inasmuch as descriptions come from some describer's analysis, elements of the description belong to the describer. It is the *description* that includes the characteristic "enmeshed"; enmeshment is not the family's characteristic. Descriptions are like maps and menus: They are real in that they exist, yet the picture they provide may be of questionable accuracy. The description is always at *a different logical level* than that which it describes.

In terms of families, differentiating family interaction from the term that we use to describe it helps us to avoid thinking that *families* are "pathological," or "chaotic," or "devitalized." Also, differentiation allows us to see, with Dell (1982), that "homeostasis," "rules," and "family boundaries" are merely parts of our description, not properties of families.

In the development of family theory, and less formal thinking about families, many typologies have been created. Cuber and Harroff's (1963) five kinds of families, the O'Neills' (1972) "open" and "closed" families, and the circumplex model (Olson et al., 1979) are just three examples of typologies that are widely used in analyzing, describing, and understanding families. These typologies have helped us to think about families.

There is no doubt about the value of these typologies; we are not arguing that they have no place. Our point is only that families are the way they are; they just exist, and their interaction processes simply occur; it is the *analyst who describes* what he sees and puts the perceived interaction into some *preestablished category*. Families act without categories; the names of family processes are supplied by observers.

Accuracy is greatly increased if, instead of saying something like "The family is enmeshed," we say:

A. I would put that family into a category labelled "enmeshed."
B. Some of the interaction processes of that family indicate to me that the members are enmeshed. Specifically, these processes include . . ."
C. I believe that the best word to describe how that family works is "enmeshed."

Each of the above indicates clearly that the term belongs to the describer rather than to the described and, as such, each statement invites further discussion and consideration. When we say "The family is enmeshed," the subject tends to become closed and further discussion is less likely.

8. *Think "fit" rather than "cause."*

For many reasons, the idea of cause continues to influence the way people consider human behavior. Since we have indicated our preference for "fit," we are obligated to indicate the problems that we believe attend causal thinking. Inasmuch as problems with the idea of cause are many and the idea of fit is central to our inquiry, this section will be lengthy.

The word "cause" carries baggage from its prior pivotal position in the physical sciences. These accretions include the idea of determinism, the idea that creative internal processes do not exist. For example, when a billiard ball at rest is struck by a billiard ball in motion, the former's position and velocity change and this change is caused by the force of the moving ball. The resting ball has virtually no effect on the speed or direction of the approaching ball. Neither ball has experience of former interaction. Neither ball has any choice in the matter and both are devoid of mental process. We say that one ball causes the other to move or to stop or to change direction.

When "cause" is moved into the social science realm it carries with it these physical science ideas. This deterministic inference is carried even though the meaning of the word is changed so that in social sciences it means something like "affect."

In the following, we will first consider "cause" in social science and then consider the less extreme case of "affect." "Affect" is synonomous with "act on" and we use it as the verb of which "effect" is the nounal counterpart. We do not use "affect" in the psychological sense (*af*-fect) of "emotional tie" or "feeling."

Cause. There are some people who borrow "cause" in an undiluted form from the physical sciences. They believe that "cause" means that one person can determine how another person will behave and that this causality is usual in normal human interaction. This thinking is reflected in such statements as "You make me so mad," and "Her husband drove her to having an affair." It is our contention that such thinking reflects a deficient view of social reality. The deficiency emanates from three erroneous assumptions: first, that the recipient of some treatment has only one way to respond to that treatment; secondly, that the recipient has no creative ability to generate alternative solutions; and third, that the recipient of the treatment has no effect on the treatment giver.

We believe that the first assumption is erroneous because reflection leads us to believe that sometimes we act differently than at other times even though we are faced with the same interactional problem. Consider the variability of a person's reactions to obnoxious automobile drivers. Sometimes a person will ignore a driver's inconsiderate behavior, and at other times he will respond truculently. The external event is virtually the same; it is the person's feelings or mood or sense of self that varies and these *internal properties contribute more* to a person's response than does the other driver's provocation.

Our experience tells us that the second assumption, that alternatives cannot be created, is incorrect. As recipients of another's aggression, or of another's pity, or some other behavior that we have not appreciated, we have considered alternatives and we have developed new responses and new solutions to problems. Frequently, the development of new responses and new solutions is called *growth*.

We only need to appeal to our sense of the world to see the error in the third assumption. Linear cause can only mean that "Alan causes Bob to behave in a particular way and that Alan acts independently of anything that Bob might do." However, we believe that Alan cannot be "the cause" of Bob's behavior inasmuch as Bob exists as part of the context in which Alan's initial behavior occurred. (If Bob were not present, Alan could have no affect on him.) Since Alan cannot affect Bob without Bob being present, and since Alan's behavior is affected by this presence, Alan's behavior is to some degree dependent on what Bob does or has done. With "some dependence" there is not the absolute independence for Alan that "cause" requires.

Taking an extreme situation, consider an adult's attempting to control a child's life completely, starting at infancy. The argument for "cause" would be that the adult causes the child to behave in a particular way and makes the child into either an exemplary adult or into a person who is not able to behave competently in ordinary society. In the second case, believers in linear causality would say that the adult causes the child's behavior to be disturbed.

For them to be correct, their argument would have to contain the following elements. First, they would have to show that the adult's behavior was not at all affected by the child. Second, they would have to show that the adult was the only socializer of the child. Third, they would have to predict exactly what type of disturbed behavior (or behavior showing competence) would be the outcome of the process.

Linear thinkers could not do the first because the adult would have to arrange his schedule to coincide with the child's time of most receptivity. The adult's socializing techniques would have to be adapted to those which would work most effectively for that particular child.[8] In other ways as well, the adult would be affected by the child (or more accurately, would be affected by the interplay between the child's behavior and the adult's plan for the child). The adult's behavior and the child's behavior would thereby be inextricably linked.

Those maintaining that the adult causes the child's behavior would also have to prove that the child was restricted to that one adult for his socialization.[9] In this extreme and unreal case, it might be possible to limit a child to just one socializer, but in the real world, this is extremely unlikely to happen for an extended period of time.

And, even if the situation of a single socializer were to occur, the way that the child would turn out is far from predictable. "Mental disturbance" or "mental well-being" could possibly be predicted in some gross and general sense but the exact place on the continuum between "health" and "ill-health" could hardly be accurately stipulated before the child-adult interaction began. Also, the behavioral areas in which this particular level of health would be made manifest and those areas in which disturbed thinking would not be found, could not be specified beforehand. Therefore, for these reasons—our experience of our own variable responses, our ability to generate new solutions, the reality of mutual involvement, and the impossibility of accurate prediction—we repudiate the idea of "cause" as applied to human affairs.

As another way of looking at this issue, consider the idea that systems are "structure-determined" (Maturana, 1978). Structural determinism holds that a system *can* be perturbed by some contextual aspect, but the *nature* of the perturbance is *determined by the system's structure* and not by the contextual aspect. The system's structure determines the qualities that the perturbing entity must have in order that the system be affected. Although the perturbance "triggers" change, it is the system's structure that determines the extent to which the system's patterns will be changed, the particular patterns that will be revised, and the direction that the changes will take (Dell, 1985). The outside element cannot *make* a system do something that the system is structurally incapable of doing.

Dell (1985) comes directly to the point. In explaining why "cause" cannot appropriately be applied to systems, he says that:

> [With "cause"] A unilaterally determines how B will respond: a professor's lecture causes every student in the class to attain an identical understanding and, thereby, identical answers on their examinations. . . . Thus, when Maturana says that causality is impossible, he means that the professor's lecture did not determine the response of his students . . . (p. 8)

Dell goes on to say that the professor's lecture "selected" the student's response but that it was the student's structure that determined the way that she responded. He then likens the association between the professor's "selection" and the student's response to getting a can of pop out of a Coke machine. Although a person gets a Sprite when they push the "Sprite" button, the selector has not "caused" the machine to provide the Sprite. The person has only selected "the response of the machine . . . but (pushing the button) does not determine that the machine gives . . . a Sprite when the button is pushed" as that determination is provided by the internal structure of the machine.

Getting rid of the idea of "cause" is easier said than done for the reason that ideas of "cause" and "control" are part of the personality and thought structure of contemporary North Americans. Most people strongly believe that they can "make" somebody do something and/or that they can "control" the way that another person behaves. These beliefs are so strongly held that arguments to the contrary are virtually ineffectual.

A paradox has been created. We, the authors, are attempting to "control" your (reader's) thinking and/or "cause" you to hold a different set of beliefs. Everything that we do will be ineffective if our ideas run counter to your personality structure and the structure of your thinking. Obviously, our (authors') problem is that we are attempting to "control" your thinking and get you to see that "control" is impossible. Your problem (if you continue to hold to the idea of "cause" and "control") is to harmonize your idea that control is possible with your thinking which is impervious to our strong arguments.[10] So, we will no longer attempt to change your thought structure; we will only suggest that you understand the importance of what we are attempting to say.

Affect. We have presented an argument against "cause." We will now consider the advantages of using "affect" rather than "cause."[11]

For those persons for whom "cause" and "affect" are synonomous, we suggest that "affect" be used for the reason that clarity is promoted by using words without baggage from other usages. And, although we cannot cause another person to act in a certain way, we can affect what they do.

Effect varies. First, there is indirect effect. If I change my way of relating to another person, that person's behavior will change to accommodate my revised action. If I act in a friendlier fashion, he may either define my behavior as improved and become more friendly or he may become more watchful of me if he does not trust me. If I become more unpleasant, he may reject me or he may try harder to obtain my goodwill. He may act in other ways as well. At any rate, my changed behavior has led to his review of our relationship and I have thereby affected his thinking. I have also affected his observable behavior inasmuch as his moving toward me or away from me or becoming more watchful was his response to his interpretation of the prior change in me.

We can also affect another's behavior in situations in which we can either inflict pain on him or enhance his comfort. Orwell's *1984* is the classic example of the former and the academic and corporate "rat races" exemplify the latter. Certainly, the manipulation of rewards and punishments does affect the behavior of those who only possess (or think that they can only possess) that which others give them.

We can also "hook" another person by saying or doing those things that experience has taught will "get her going." We are sometimes surprised, however, when for reasons or feelings of her own, she does not rise to the bait as we anticipated. However, being able to hook someone occurs with sufficient frequency that we believe we are affecting another's behavior. And of course, sometimes we are.

So, "affect" is appropriately used in relationships of extreme complementariness (where one person dominates and the other submits) and in situations in which the affector first changes his own behavior and the affectee responds. "Affect" is also appropriate when we hook someone and they respond as we expect them to.

Even "affect" must be used with care, however. In normal family interaction, "affect" is subject to the same qualifiers as is "cause." Our affecting another's *behavior* is never totally independent of their affecting *us*. We are never (or very rarely) the only person in another's life and therefore other persons and other experiences are part of the context of interaction. We are never sure how the other person will react to our attempt to affect his actions. Our behavior toward others only *proposes* that they change; it is their structure that determines their adaptation: Our behavior proposes, their structure disposes. With those qualifiers, the use of "affect" can make sense; without the qualifiers, "affect" assumes more one-way control than is warranted.

Think "fit" rather than "affect." Dell (1982) has made a strong case for the use of the word "fit" in describing systemic interaction. "Without making reference to the etiology of causation, fit simply posits that the behaviors in a family system have a general complementarity; they fit together" (p. 21). Ideas related to "fit" and "general complementarity imply" no interpretation of either the nature or direction of interaction; there is no assumption of causality or affect, mutual

or otherwise. Fit then, is more appropriate than either cause
or affect in being applied to what happens in living systems.

The importance of the distinction between "fit" and "cause."
The importance of the discussion of fit and causality should
not be underestimated; this is not merely an intellectual game
that we are engaged in here. The idea that the notion of
causation can be applied in human relations is the basis of
much grief in the world today at the international level in
the "family of nations," in therapeutic situations, and in our
personal affairs. The standoff-without-remedy of relations between the United States and the Soviet Union is based on an
idea held and advanced by each nation's leaders. That idea
is that, "*we* are guiltless, we are only responding to *their* arming.
They are causing our behavior." Each nation sees that what
it does is separate from what the other does and that its
actions are caused by the actions of the other. A systems
view would see, not two systems, but a single system in which
each superpower plays its part and each part that is played
incorporates and then extends the part played by the other.
The situation is not one of linear cause and effect, it is one
of fit.

In therapy, help cannot be given by a therapist to a family
if the therapist believes that "the wife causes the husband to
act" in some particular way. The therapist, to be helpful,
must see the part that each plays in maintaining a relationship
which neither wants but to which both parties have become
accustomed. In relationships that continue over time, the
therapist who attempts to get one party to change will be
ineffective unless the other's behavior and the interaction of
all concerned are considered.

Finally, in our own lives, unless we divest ourselves of
self-serving rationalizations based upon the idea that we are
helpless victims, we can never extricate ourselves from harmful
interactional situations. Unless we maintain the idea that we
have a hand in making our own lives, we are stuck and
constrained to take what others give us. The crucial question
becomes, "What am I doing that affects her and promotes
the continuation of a situation in which her behavior fits with
mine?" Asking that, we may be able to change our own

behavior (or withdraw) and thereby change the interaction and the other person's actions.

Personal responsibility and the systems view. Before leaving this issue of cause and effect, there is one further issue which bears consideration. Systems analysis holds the idea that the behavior of each family member fits with that of other family members. This fit seems to imply the existence of intrafamilial monolithic patterns in which the person's behavior plays only a small part. It does not take too much effort to extend this line of thought to the point that personal responsibility for actions is eliminated. For example, a person might well say, "Systems thinking indicates that I acted in a particular way because of the family's interaction patterns. In fact, I had no *choice* but to do what I did because everyone in the family was pressuring (or encouraging, or allowing) me to do it. So, don't blame me, I am just a part of a larger system and my behavior, although you don't like it, is the only kind of behavior that was possible, given the system's organization and its power."

Let us suppose that the behavior in question is a father's sexual abuse of his daughter. We will consider the father's responsibility for his behavior within the systems perspective as we interpret that perspective.

Whether or not such a stance (shifting blame to the family) can be morally justified is not the issue here (we think that it cannot); our concern is whether or not such a stance can be *theoretically* justified within the systems framework. A way to resolve the problem would be to apply the appropriate rules that we established earlier.

To apply the first rule, the system being considered should be defined. The system being considered is the person and not the family, and the behavior being justified is a person's behavior and not a system's behavior. A family cannot sexually abuse a child; a father can, however. If we confine our consideration to the father, family interaction patterns are irrelevant.

The second rule, that which concerns the use of inter-action language rather than the language of the physical sciences, is also helpful. A paraphrase of the person's rationalization is that "the family caused my behavior." That expression reflects physical science thinking and not thinking associated with creatively interacting systems. We maintain the existence and the importance of choice in mindful systems and we see the justification of behavior by the elimination of choice as being a part of some other theory, not this one.

Moving on quickly, "the family made me do it" is a nonexplanation (Rule 3), for it begs the important questions of "How exactly did the family 'make you' do it?"; "What part of the family made you do it?"; "How did the family as a whole make you do it?" and so forth.

A related idea (from Rule 6) is that the person who has blamed his family is not allowing for his own influence on the family. He has theoretically *separated* himself from the family by saying that the family has made him do something and then he has made himself a non-separable part of the family by indicating that his behavior is merely a part of the whole. Clearly, this is a weak position and he can not have it both ways. Either he is a part of the system and, in that case, he affects family interaction and contributes to that which happens in the family; his contribution includes his input into his own abusive behavior. Or, he is a separate entity and, in this case, his actions do not necessarily fit with the actions of other family members. As a separate entity, he must take full responsibility.

A related and equally non-systemic argument is frequently made on the other side of the issue. Systems theory is criticized for holding a family member responsible (or even for "blaming" that member) for that which occurs to her in a family. For example, critics say that systems theory indicates that a wife could be blamed for being battered because the theory indicates that each family member contributes to that which occurs in the family system. So, if there is spousal violence in the family, the battered spouse is partially responsible for her own battering.

Since this is an extremely sensitive issue, we will take great care in expressing our position on wife abuse and systems theory. Moreover, we trust that readers will be equally careful in reading what we have to say. Our point is that systems theory neither absolves the abusing husband nor blames the victim. On the contrary, we believe that systems theory can be helpful in understanding wife abuse[12] and this help comes from three uses of the theory.

First, as the work of Murray Straus and his colleagues (Straus, 1980; Straus, Gelles, & Steinmetz, 1980) has indicated, rates of wife abuse are related to social factors. For example, the relationship between the cultural acceptance of violence and wife abuse is positive: the greater the acceptance, as in time of war, the more abuse.

This makes sense in the systems perspective in that the systems view holds that what happens anywhere in a social system is related to that which happens someplace else. Our application of the systems perspective holds that if you wish to reduce family violence, you will need to reduce all kinds of violence. That includes capital punishment, war, sports violence, corporal punishment of children in schools and homes, and depictions of violence in magazines, on television, and in films.

The systems perspective can also be useful in understanding violence when it is applied to the personality system of the abuser. At the personal system level, the abusing husband can be described as pathological, sadistic, stupid, or drunk. The wife abuser can be reacting to his own internal needs and the source of these needs can be totally unrelated to his wife's personality, behavior, or even to her presence. She need only be there as an object for his use. From this perspective, wife abuse is a sign of the abuser's pathology and this is true even if the abuse is said to have been provoked by the wife.

We have so far indicated that wife abuse reflects social violence and indicates personal pathology. Since this book is about family systems, social elements and personal psychology are side issues. The question that still remains is: What does family systems theory say about family violence? Our answer is that there are sources of family violence that are neither social nor personal. Some cases of abuse can only be understood if we first acknowledge that they *have their source in and draw their momentum from* dysfunctional family patterns. In cases of this type, both spouses are involved, both have input. Note that we referred to *source and momentum:* The violent end to the episode must always be the responsibility of the abuser as an individual.

How can this be? How can an abused wife contribute to a violent episode? Systems theory indicates that family interaction has its own dynamics and that violence is sometimes the extension of ordinary conflict into extraordinary and extreme interactional sequences. In a violent episode, one thing leads to another. There is the intensification of feelings, personal and vitriolic verbal attacks are made and the abuser loses control of his temper and associated behavior.

As an isolated episode, the beating of the wife by the husband includes no contribution of the wife: The abuse is a matter of the strong beating the weak. However, as a repeated interactional sequence in a continuing relationship, the matter takes on a different character. If abuse is repeated in a relationship, it may be that the wife plays a part in maintaining the abusive pattern.[13] The contributions that she makes to the family have the effect of continuing the spousal relationship and, if abuse is an integral part of spousal interaction, then, in a sense, she supports the continuation of the abuse. Indeed, persons working with battered wives have indicated that one of the most heartbreaking parts of this helping activity occurs when an abused woman is unable to remain steadfast and apart from her husband. By returning to him she stops withholding her contribution to the relationship, the very withholding that serves to change the system and thereby make a better life for her.

Finally, our view of systems theory includes the idea that systems include processes that emerge from the interaction of the parts. These processes are not characteristic of the parts taken individually and, moreover, the processes have lives of their own.[14] For example, Alice and Bob will establish a unique pattern of interaction and, although neither Alice nor Bob is violent or even particularly conflictual with others, the mix of their personalities generates clashes. These clashes may escalate to violence due to the unwillingness of either one to give in. It may be that "unwillingness" is in reality "inability" because their interactional repertoire includes neither yielding nor the acceptance of yielding.

On the other hand, Arthur and Brenda might have a more traditional arrangement and Brenda takes a subordinate position in all things. Violence could be associated with Arthur's attempts to intimidate Brenda and thereby remind her of her lower status, or it could be associated with her attempts to change the relationship to one that includes more mutuality.

These two different kinds of relationships illustrate an important point that has two parts. The major point is that an understanding of violence in the relationships of Alice and Bob and Brenda and Arthur requires the consideration of each couple's *relationship interaction*. The first sub-point is that consideration of either the social context or the participants' personalities will allow only a partial understanding of the complexities surrounding the violence. This is true because the source and momentum of violence is to be found in each couple's interaction; the source and momentum are not to be found in either social context or personal ill health. A view of violence which does not include interaction patterns will yield only an incomplete picture of what is happening.

The second sub-point is that a consideration of family interaction is necessary if differences in types of violence are to be noted. Clearly, the two couples have substantial differences in their interaction patterns and their violence is different in source, meaning, and function. To see these two types of violence as identical is to perceive inaccurately; to treat them identically is to err.

Therapy based on this type of systems analysis would attempt immediately to stop the beating, change the abusive behavior of the husband, and assist the wife in discontinuing behavior that helps maintain the relationship that includes her abuse. In the case of escalating violence, such as Alice and Bob, the couple's interactional repertoire needs to be increased by the addition and acceptance of yielding or forbearing behavior. In cases in which violence is used to subjugate, the relationship repertoire should be increased by the addition and acceptance of mutuality and competitiveness.[15]

Summary. In keeping with the ideas so far expressed regarding cause and effect, systems theorists have replaced "linear cause" with "mutual cause." This does not solve the problem for, as Dell says, "mutual cause" is a flawed idea that should be replaced, in the interests of logical consistency, with the idea of "fit" (Dell, 1982). The idea of mutual cause is inconsistent with the systems view because it requires that the continuous interaction that exists within a system be made discontinuous. For example, Bob and Alan do not cause each other's behavior ("mutual cause"); Bob and Alan contribute to interaction sequences which include what each does. With the systems view, a system's processes are continuous and they are extensions of previous interaction. Any kind of "cause," even "mutual cause," freezes the family's ongoing process and incorrectly posits a beginning to some interaction sequence (Watzlawick, Beavin, & Jackson, 1967).

The idea of "fit" or "mesh" avoids such errors. "Without making reference to etiology or causation, fit simply posits that the behaviors occurring in the family system have a general complementarity" (Dell, 1982, p. 21).

In the example in "Rule 6," regarding the family's pattern deficiencies and the child's mental disturbance, an appropriate rewriting would read: "The family's particular interaction patterns meshed with the child's behavior." With this rewriting, knowledge about whether the child's behavior "caused" the family's ineffective patterns or vice versa is not assumed. Such an assumption would exceed knowledge.[16] All that can be said with integrity is that the family's patterns and the child's behavior seem to fit together in such a way that one builds upon the other.

This principle can be used in another important way: fit is important, and ideas, as well as persons, can fit together. Systems theory fits with other ways of looking at families and its synthesis with other perspectives will make systems theory more useful in explaining family interaction. Information theory, theories of perception, communication theory, and even a humanistic perspective are all compatible with systems theory and widening the theory to embrace these other perspectives will make systems-based analysis richer, more congruent with reality, and more insightful.

These are the principles which have guided our thinking as we have developed this book. We hope that the remainder of the book will give evidence of the principles' value.

NOTES

1. We extensively explore "cause" below. See pages 30–42.

2. See Rule 5, below, for a deeper analysis of the ways that the properties of a subsystem are different from the properties of the system of which it is a part.

3. A clear statement of how Reiss and Oliveri make mind a family-level property and transform family mind (they make "paradigm" synonymous with "family mind") into a cause is the following: "As our model suggests, the character of the paradigm is a fundamental property of the family itself; it shapes the transactions of all its members with its social community" (Reiss & Oliveri, 1983, p. 90). As can be seen from this quotation, mind is a property that exists at the level of the family; cause is indicated by the use of "shapes." Moreover, they have made family mind or "paradigm" into a collectivity which has a membership, for, in the quotation, "it" must refer to paradigm, its character. Instead of family members having minds, it seems to be the other way around and the family mind has members. This quote well illustrates problems associated with maintaining the distinction between system levels.

4. Readers may find the glossary at the end of the book to be helpful. The glossary includes systems-related terms and other specialized terminology.

5. Since many of the ideas for clear thinking and writing are general and have been used for many years, no attempt will be made to indicate either an initial source or every source. We will indicate those sources that provided us with the particular idea or an especially clear statement of the idea.

6. This point is developed in more detail below; see "Change as decrease in order."

7. A system's "environment" is also called its "context."

8. Some research shows that infants contribute to the nature of parent-child interaction, and even have an impact on parents' personality (Firignano & Lachman, 1985).

9. Even if one person acted as the socializer, others would be involved because the socializer's relationships with these others affects his activities with the child. For example, Belsky's (1984) model specifies the importance of husband-wife interaction to the mother-child and father-child relationships.

10. Of course, you could say that we have been unable to control your thinking because our arguments are inadequate and weak. This, however, is just another way of saying that the arguments are unconvincing; they lack the power to convince for the reason that they do not fit with your structure of thought.

11. While "cause" can be used as either a verb or a noun, we are not as fortunate in our use of affect/effect. "Effect" is the nounal form and "affect" is used as the verb.

12. Sad experience has illustrated that there are some people who believe that even the idea that it is important "to understand" wife abuse is to make an apology for it. Their position is that we must stop wife abuse, not explain it, and that wife abusers are despicable persons who should be, in their words, shot rather than understood. Frequently, these persons are active in abused women's shelters and they have seen at first hand how women and children are destroyed by abuse. We appreciate their feelings and agree with them that abuse must cease. We disagree with their idea about the usefulness of violent punishment for abusers and we believe that understanding an objectionable phenomenon is an important first step in attempting to reduce its frequency.

13. It may be, and this is often the case, that the wife believes that she cannot remove herself from the situation and

her own dependency and/or that of her children requires that she remain in a marriage that contains violence. Obviously, if the wife is in either an economic or emotional prison, her "contribution" to the continuation of the relationship is forced and is no contribution at all.

14. Later in this book, in considerations of positive and negative feedback loops and in the discussion of complementariness and symmetry, conflict is further examined.

15. Here we are indicating what each of these systems needs in order to function without violence; we are not suggesting any particular type of therapy. We are not suggesting that in situations of domestic violence, that the husband and wife enter conjoint therapy and that they sit down in the presence of a therapist and work out their systemic problems. As Gelles and Maynard (1984) indicated, the systems approach to family violence can only be applied when the violence is either mild or moderate; conjoint therapy or systems based interventions are "clearly inappropriate and extremely dangerous" in cases of extreme and life threatening violence.

16. It could be said that family interaction patterns affect a child more than the child's personality affects the family because the family's interaction patterns existed prior to the child's appearance on the scene. On the other hand, a child cannot be affected until he is present and, with his presence, a changed system is created. This new system will, in all likelihood, affect interaction more than will the residues of former systems.

Chapter 2

"SILVER ANNIVERSARY"

A Family Entertainment

The dramatic sketch that follows is included in the book, not because of its literary value, but because it serves to illustrate what happens in families. The sketch explores a family's (the Spencers') interaction patterns using a systems perspective. Also, the sketch shows how the behavior of persons in families fits with the actions of other family members. Readers will find it helpful to read the sketch now as it will be referred to in the remainder of the book.

SILVER ANNIVERSARY
by
Jason Montgomery

A ONE-ACT DOCUMENTARY TV DRAMA

CAST:

William Spencer:	A fifty-year-old entrepreneur.
Beverly:	His wife.
Carolyn:	Their daughter, twenty-two years old.
Debbie:	A younger daughter, eighteen years of age.

CONTEXT:

The drama takes place in the kitchen of a suburban home. The Spencers are well-to-do and their new house reflects this. There are kitchen counters and cupboards and the most modern appliances. These elements give the impression of modern living and affluence and a "kitschy" level of taste. There is a table with four chairs and the day's mail is on the table.

The kitchen has two doors. The one at the left leads to the outside and the one at the right leads to other parts of the house. There is a large window or patio door in the rear wall and the part of the backyard that can be seen reflects the same level of expenditure and taste as the kitchen.

SILVER ANNIVERSARY

By Jason Montgomery

The Spencers live in an expensive suburban area. Their house is essentially similar to the other houses with no particular architectural or other uniqueness. CAMERA PANS to an approaching car and the large station wagon turns into the Spencers' driveway. The garage door opens and then closes when the car is safely inside.

(INTERIOR, SPENCERS' KITCHEN)

(Debbie and William enter through door left. Debbie goes directly to the table and starts looking through the mail. William announces their arrival.)

William: Hello, Mother, we're home.

(There is no answer. William moves to the kitchen counter on which he places his attaché case. He listens for an answer and none is forthcoming. He then moves to the table and appears interested in the mail that Debbie is looking at.)

William: Find mother, will you? And tell her I'm home.

Debbie: (somewhat unhappily) Oh, all right.

William: She's probably in the rec room, doing some cleaning for tonight.

(Debbie exits through door right. William picks up the mail which Debbie has unceremoniously dropped and begins to go through it. He appears particularly interested in one envelope and he hastily opens it.)

William: What the hell is this? Beverly!

(There is no answer.)

William: (continuing) Beverly!

(Almost immediately, Beverly enters from door right. Under an apron, she is wearing an expensive, but dowdy dress that is much too old for her.)

Beverly: You called me? I'm sorry I didn't hear you. I was doing some last-minute straightening up.

(She looks around the kitchen expectantly. When she sees the attaché case, she goes to it, opens it, and removes plastic sandwich containers and plastic spoons and other lunch stuff. She puts the plastic implements in the dishasher and puts William's attaché case in the kitchen cupboard.

William: What's this from Ester's Fashion Center?

(Beverly takes off apron and models her new dress for him. He takes no notice.)

Beverly: I had to have a new dress for a very special event.

William: (Angrily, out of patience) You broke your promise. You agreed that you wouldn't buy any expensive clothes without checking with me first. How could you do that?

Beverly: (whining) The dress *wasn't* expensive. You should have seen the prices on. . . .

William: (interrupting) You wrote a check for it. This check, and its come back marked "insufficient funds."

Beverly: (sheepishly) Oh, *no!*

William: You knew there wasn't enough money in your account to cover it, didn't you.

Beverly: I . . . I'd thought I'd cover it before it cleared but then I forgot.

William: Damn it, Beverly. Why do you do things like this?

Beverly: I don't know. (Hurriedly). I thought you wanted me to look *nice*.

Wiiliam: I do. But that's too much for a dress. *I* pay almost that much for a *suit*. And, what's more, the check bounced. I *keep* telling you! You can only spend money you have.

Beverly: I knew you'd be furious but it looked so good on me that I just couldn't refuse. I do so want to look nice for this special occasion.

(During her last statement, Beverly starts to breathe irregularly).

William: (finally realizes that she is wearing the dress) It is nice. I guess it's worth it. It really does look nice. I'll be real proud of you.

Beverly: Thank you, dear. I really wanted you to like it.

William: I'll straighten out the check business for you. But, I still expect you to clear big expenses with me. We had enough problems before with stuff like this and we don't want you to get in trouble again.

(Beverly gets gin from the cupboard and begins to make martinis. William sits down and continues to look through the mail.)

Beverly: Did things go okay today?

William: Hm? Damn government. I worked on payroll and unemployment insurance and witholding-tax the whole bloody day.

Beverly: Couldn't Debbie do that?

William: Not very likely. She's good for some things but this has to be done just right.

(Beverly finishes making a pitcher of martinis and she pours two. She puts the glasses and the pitcher on a tray and serves the drinks.)

William: (matter-of-factly) To Mr. and Mrs. Spencer on their silver wedding anniversary.

Beverly: To *us!*

(They drink silently. Beverly indicates the cards that William has been opening.)

Beverly: (continuing) It looks like we got several anniversary cards today.

William: Yes. Here's one from the Cargills. One from your brother. The Barnes. (Pause.) The Simpsons. They're in Greece. The Cunninghams.

Beverly: (holding on to the Simpsons' card) Remember the fun we used to have with the Simpsons? When they'd call us and we'd put a picnic lunch together and drive to the beach? And then we'd spend all afternoon there, just sitting in the sun and talking.

William: (regretfully) That was certainly a long time ago. Somehow things were different then. You know what I mean? (Pause.) We haven't been to the shore in years. Not since I bought the business.

Beverly: It was just a stage in life. A kind of daredevil stage.

William: Nose to the grindstone, that's us.

Beverly: (vacantly) I don't regret it. We made something of ourselves.

(William continues to open cards, to look at them, to pass them to Beverly one at a time. Silence.)

William: I didn't think we'd get so many.

Beverly: It must be that people recognize the ideal marriage.

William: (not quite convinced) That must be it.

(They drink quietly. Beverly remembers something and jumps up quickly and goes to the refrigerator. She gets canapés and puts them on the table.)

Beverly: The caterers dropped off the appetizers. Try one, dear. They're good.

(William eats one and they resume their quiet drinking. Beverly jumps up and checks on the food in the oven.)

William: Will you sit down?

Beverly: I only want things to be perfect.

William: I know, sweetheart, and they are. The place never looked better.

(Silence. William looks at his drink. Beverly looks at the cards.)

Beverly: How much time do we have?

William: Crosby's are always early. They should be here soon. (Pause.) It's been good.

Beverly: Yes.

William: I mean our marriage.

Beverly: I know. (Pause.) Twenty-five years. It hardly seems possible. Twenty-five years ago tonight.

(William takes jewelry case from his pocket and walks around Beverly while she sits there expectantly. He places a pendant around her neck.)

William: For you, sweetheart. Because you're so wonderful.

(Beverly gets a mirror and admires herself.)

Beverly: Oh, William. It's beautiful.

William: I'm glad you like it.

Beverly: I do, oh, I really do. And it's from Jordan's.

(They embrace, a bit stiffly.)

William: I guess you really deserve it. Putting up with a dictator like me.

Beverly: Don't be silly. We've been good for each other.

William: It looks really nice with your dress. (Pause.) Another drink? I'll make these.

(Beverly finishes her drink quickly, makes a face of distaste and gives her glass to William.)

Beverly: I'll have another one, just like the other one.

(They smile wanly at the worn-out joke. William pours drinks for each from the pitcher that Beverly had previously used. Beverly looks at herself in the mirror and leaves the mirror on the table.)

William: We've been through a lot together. Three houses, the business, the children.

(Pause.)

Beverly: Sometimes it wasn't easy.

(Beverly waits for a response but none is forthcoming.)

Beverly: (continuing) The struggle was worth it, though. Don't you think?

William: Remember the long hours I had to put in when I was getting the business started?

Beverly: And how Carolyn and I used to bring hot suppers for you?

William: (surprised) Er, yes. That too. That was a real partnership.

Beverly: We were really fortunate, having something to do together. A common goal like that. Something to look forward to.

William: You're right. You were a big help.

(Pause.)

Beverly: A penny for your thoughts.

William: I wonder what would have happened if you hadn't inherited the money.

Beverly: I don't know. What do you mean?

William: I mean, if we hadn't bought the business, where would we be right now? Like the Simpsons, having a good time in Greece or just having time for ourselves right here. What would the last twenty years have been like, I wonder.

Beverly: We wouldn't be on easy street, that's one thing.

(Pause.)

William: Do you ever think about us? Our lives. The way we are?

Beverly: Oh, sure. Lots. And when I do, I thank my lucky stars for letting me have what I wanted—this house, this husband, this family. I like being married to a successful man.

(She extends her hand to William who slowly takes it. They are quiet. After a time, they both start to talk at once. Beverly stops.)

William: You have everything under control for tonight?

Beverly: Oh, yes. The caterer has dropped off several thngs. There will be three people serving drinks at eight-thirty. Oh, Lord, the glasses.

William: What about them?

Beverly: Debbie was supposed to pick them up.

(She looks through the cupboards.)

Beverly: Where would she put them?

William: She didn't get them. She said she told you.

Beverly: Well, she didn't. Oh, William. What are we going to do? How can we have a party with no glasses?

(She begins to wheeze.)

William: Don't get upset now. There has got to be an easy solution. I know! We can call the Hastings. They can stop by the church and pick some up on their way over.

Beverly: Well, I guess that will be all right.

William: Of course it is. We have enough for awhile and then the Hastings will be here.

Beverly: Thank you. You're such a dear. Still, it's something that Debbie should have done.

William: Stop fretting. She must have forgotten. She's been working hard lately. Anyway, it's all settled. Is everything else okay?

Beverly: I think so. I have the food, the ice. The house is ready.

William: Good. Now you relax until the guests arrive.

(Pause. William picks out a card, the Simpsons' card, and stares at it. Beverly is nervous about something, quite agitated, and William is impervious. Finally she comes out with it.)

Beverly: I've been thinking about something a lot today.

William: Umm?

Beverly: Remember when we were first married? We set our goals—a house like this, a good income, children, a lifetime of happiness as husband and wife?

William: Yes?

Beverly: And we planned on grandchildren nearby. A life complete.

William: Well, we've done all that. Except for the grand-children, that is.

Beverly: Yes. And in this whole lovely picture, the only bad part is Carolyn.

William: She's a bad part, all right. I'm glad you finally agree.

Beverly: It's so sad. That way she left. I feel really bad about her. When she ran away, I felt that we had failed.

William: What malarkey. She's just no good. An ingrate, that's all.

Beverly: Will, it would be so nice to have her near us. We could let bygones be bygones. We could say we did everything that we set out to do.

William: I don't know what you're driving at, but whatever it is, you can just forget it. I don't want her around. We don't even know where she is.

Beverly: But we do.

William: What do you mean?

Beverly: She lives in Toronto. Debbie even talked to her.

William: When did all this happen? How?

Beverly: Debbie asked her to come tonight.

William: Carolyn coming here? Tonight? Are you kidding me? No. You're not, are you. This is serious.

Beverly: Oh, William. Don't be angry. (Excited) I do so want to see her. (whining) It means more to me than anything else. We can't reject her just because she made some mistakes. She's our daughter and this is her home. I want her here where she belongs.

William: You want her here?

Beverly: More than anything. To stay. I want her to come home.

William: Good God! I don't believe this. After that meat grinder she put you through? Don't you remember? Even if she comes, she won't stay and you'll go through it all again.

Beverly: It will be all right. You'll see. I'm better now. I won't get sick again, I promise. Please, Will? It's really important to me. Let it be an anniversary gift.

(She coughs, almost as a warning.)

William: You'll be sorry, is all I can say. (aside) This is stupid and there's not a goddam thing I can do about it. (more directly to Beverly) Are you sure she's coming?

Beverly: She told Debbie that she would try.

William: When did you hear from her? How is she getting here?

Beverly: I don't know. Debbie talked to her. She told Debbie that she didn't know if she was coming or not and that she couldn't promise. Carolyn said she didn't know if she'd be welcome.

William: That makes two of us. (Pause.) It sounds to me like you don't know very much about it, even if she's coming or not.

Beverly: If my prayers are answered, she'll be here.

(Debbie enters from door right. It is obvous that Debbie is unhappy; her obesity and sloppiness both advertise and aggravate her listlessness and depression. She gets a glass and helps herself to a very large martini which she drinks with the dedication of an alcoholic. In the course of the ensuing discussion she drinks heavily, making additional martinis as needed.)

Debbie: What were you saying about me?

William: (too quickly) Nothing. Nothing at all.

Debbie: Oh. I thought I heard my name.

Beverly: No, dear. You must have just imagined it. (Pause.) Actually, we were discussing your sister.

Debbie: (brightening) Have you heard from her?

Beverly: Not yet. But we're still hopeful.

William: Mother hopes we will, I hope we won't. What do you hope?

Debbie: I would like us to be a happy family—

Beverly: (breaking in) There. You see?

Debbie: —and really enjoy the celebration.

William: And that's what I want, too.

Beverly: (relieved) We all want the same thing. Yes, we'll all be happy tonight. As usual.

(Debbie moves to the table and gets a canapé.)

Beverly: If we just had something to drink from.

William: Mother thought you were going to pick up the glasses.

Debbie: I couldn't get to the church. I tried. I told you all this before. I said I couldn't get them.

Beverly: I know you said you were having trouble but I thought you could help at least that much.

Debbie: I'm sorry.

William: It's all right, Debbie. You have been working much too hard. You just didn't have the time. The Hastings can bring the glasses when they come.

Debbie: I told her I couldn't get them.

(Debbie gets another canapé. She gets still another and eats it in a very sloppy manner.)

Beverly: Would you like a napkin, dear?

Debbie: Yes.

(Beverly gets a napkin for her.)

Beverly: (brightly) Father and I were trying just now to remember some things. Remember when we lived on School Street? And we just had the one bathroom?

(Debbie nods. She has heard all this before.)

Beverly: (prompting) Do you remember the schedule we had?

Debbie: Sure. Dad always used the bathroom first because he had to go to work. You would go second and use it quickly and then wake us up and you'd fix breakfast while Dad got dressed. Then Carolyn and I would use the bathroom and we'd all eat breakfast together and that's how the day would start.

William: It wasn't always that way. That was only on the days that I worked. The other days I took a later turn.

Beverly: Back then you worked every day but Christmas.

Debbie: And Easter and Thanksgiving and New Year's.

William: And most Sundays.

(Pause.)

Beverly: I'm glad you don't have to work so hard anymore. We can enjoy ourselves more now.

William: I'm all for that. Let's have another drink.

(Beverly pours out drinks for her and William.)

William: (continuing) Mother tells me you've been in touch with Carolyn. I was quite surprised.

Debbie: That was the idea. Mother thought you would like a nice surprise. (dreamily) Letting bygones be bygones. The whole family together.

Beverly: (quickly) I only thought that we could show everyone just how terrific we Spencers are.

William: (to Debbie) It upsets me to think you went behind my back.

Debbie: Don't be silly. How else could we surprise you?

William: Well, I guess that's right. I hope she behaves herself.

Debbie: Of course she will. Carolyn's okay. Everyone was just trying too hard last year and things got all mixed up. But Carolyn loves you and you love her and it will be good when we are all together again. You'll see.

William: (resigned, to Beverly) Is her room all ready?

Debbie: Her room is always ready. Every week Mother changes the sheets whether anyone sleeps in them or not.

Beverly: (ignoring Debbie) Yes. It's clean and dusted. It's just like it was when she lived at home.

William: I think it will be all right if we leave those boxes of books in the closet.

Beverly: I moved them up to the attic already.

Debbie: Why did you do that? She'll only be here a night. Or two at the most.

(There is an awkward silence.)

Beverly: We might want her to stay a little longer.

(More discomfort.)

Debbie: (agitated) She has to go back. She can't stay here. She has a job and she has to go back to work.

Beverly: You don't know. She might want to come home for a while. There's nothing for her in Toronto that isn't here. She might just as well stay. Live here and work. At least we should make it easy for her if that's what she wants.

William: We've always made it easy for her to do what she wants. And now, she can come and go as she pleases, no matter what anyone else wants.

Beverly: Will, she's had a bad time in Toronto. She's lonely there. She really wants to see us all again, to come home for an evening. Our evening. And celebrate our success with us. Does that sound like so much?

(There is a pause in the conversation. Debbie attempts to get another drink but the pitcher is empty so she proceeds to make some more.)

Beverly: Don't you think you've had enough Debbie, dear?

Debbie: (Continuing to make more drinks.) Oh, I don't know.

Beverly: There's a big evening ahead, you know.

Debbie: Don't worry about me.

William: (to Beverly) Debbie is all right, we can always depend on her.

Debbie: (a toast) Here's to good old dependable Debbie.

Beverly: (to William) Of course. I didn't mean she was drinking too much or anything.

William: No. You didn't, I'm sure. We are all adults; we can all take care of ourselves.

(Pause.)

Debbie: You know, Carolyn seemed to really want to come home. For the party. But I don't know about her staying on. (to Beverly) I didn't know that's what you were thinking about.

William: Don't feel bad. I didn't even know she was coming. It's like that around here. Sometimes.

Beverly: (cheerily) Let's just wait and see. We don't even know if she'll come. Let's just have a fine time and enjoy ourselves tonight. Tomorrow will take care of itself. (Pause.) Oh, where is everyone.

(Pause.) Come on, William. Let's take a look around and make sure that everything's all set.

(William and Beverly leave the kitchen through door right, closing it as they go.)

(Debbie is alone in the kitchen. She gets a plate and puts several canapés on it and sits down at the table with the food and her drink. There is a tapping at the back door, door left. Carolyn enters and there is a warm greeting. Hugs. Laughter.)

Debbie: Care!

Carolyn: Deb!

Debbie: I'll get Mom and Dad.

Carolyn: No. Wait. Let's talk for a minute.

Debbie: But they'll want to see you. They're anxious about you.

Carolyn: Sit for a minute with me. (Pause.) How have you been?

Debbie: Not bad. In fact, really good. (reluctant to talk) Want something to eat?

Carolyn: How about I give you a hand with that?

Debbie: Okay.

(They eat together.)

Debbie: I'm really glad you came for tonight.

Carolyn: It's really nice to be here. Just the two of us.

(There is silence. Carolyn takes in the scene and she is taken aback by the drink and Debbie's appearance.)

Debbie: Don't say it. Please don't say it. I don't want to hear it from you. I know I look terrible.

Carolyn: I got the idea when you phoned me that you weren't doing very well.

Debbie: You could tell that? It was that obvious?

Carolyn: Don't forget, I'm your sister. I know you very well. Beneath the happy talk I heard that things weren't right. I got worried about you so I came to see you. Will you tell me what's happening!

Debbie: That's just it. *Nothing* is happening. I don't do much anymore. I just sit around the house and eat and watch TV. God, I hate to have you see me like this.

Carolyn: You mean you're not at university?

Debbie: I quit last spring. It was so boring. The stuff I had to learn was stupid. The students were dumb and the professors were just plain dull. You know? It just got to be a drag. I hated it, you know? You know what I mean?

Carolyn: Not exactly. Is this any better?

Debbie: (getting defensive) I work part-time so at least I feel like I'm doing something.

Carolyn: Great! Where do you work? What do you do?

Debbie: I work with Dad, doing special things for him. If there's something he needs, I go get it. Something he wants done, I do it for him.

Carolyn: You sound like Mother. She takes care of him at home and you take care of him at work.

Debbie: You know Dad. You know how hard he works. He gets to thinking about the business and he forgets to take care of himself. He needs all the help he can get.

Carolyn: How much work is there for you?

Debbie: Sometimes I help a lot, other times there is nothing. Then I just mess around. Sometimes all afternoon. Once in a while I don't do anything all day. It's really exciting.

Carolyn: Does he pay you?

Debbie: A little, for all the time I'm there. I keep track of my hours and we settle up every month.

Carolyn: Will you save enough to go back to university?

Debbie: No problem. If I want to go back, they'll support me just like they supported you.

Carolyn: You mean you might not go back?

Debbie: It doesn't matter one way or the other. I might be a dropout. What's wrong?

Carolyn: It seems like such a waste. You were doing so well before.

Debbie: (a bit sarcastic) It surely must have been due to the shining example you set.

Carolyn: (taken aback) That's not what I meant. It sounds as though you're planning to not go back and I'm dissappointed. That's all.

Debbie: (sarcastically) I'm *sorry.* I don't want to talk about it anymore.

Carolyn: But I came all this way to find out about you. I really want to know.

Debbie: You should have saved yourself the trip. (Pause.) Maybe later. I can't tell you any more right now.

Carolyn: But I have to know.

Debbie: If it's so important to you, you should have stuck around. (getting angry) I've told you all there is. All your other questions, the ones you haven't asked yet, forget them. It won't end well. You'll ask a question and I'll give you some stupid answer. You'll be "disappointed" and have a long face, and then you'll try to make me feel bad.

Carolyn: I won't try to make you feel bad.

Debbie: But I *will*. Let's just leave it. The bare facts are these: *Here* I am in this house. I live here. I watch TV here. I eat and sleep here. The only people I can depend on are here. Here I am and here I will remain. Save the sympathy. This isn't so bad. In fact, I've come to like it.

Carolyn: You just have to get out. If you don't want to go back to school, do something else. Get a real job. Or travel. Do something with your life. (Pause.) This isn't doing any good. Oh, Debbie, let's not fight. (Pause.) Let's talk about something else.

(They exchange reassuring smiles. There is a pause.)

Debbie: You know? They're still mad about your running off.

Carolyn: I guessed they were. That's why I was surprised when you called.

Debbie: It was all Mother's idea. Dad didn't even know about it until tonight.

Carolyn: That's just great!

Debbie: And there's more. Mother wants you to stay.

Carolyn: To stay?

Debbie: To move back.

Carolyn: So *that's* it!

Debbie: What's it?

Carolyn: I just couldn't figure it out. I knew they were still angry and then, all of a sudden, I got your call. It didn't make any sense. But now I know. It's because Mother wants me to come home to stay. Well, I can't. I won't.

Debbie: That's what I told them. I said you'd have to go back, that you had a job. That was right, wasn't it?

Carolyn: Of course. I couldn't move back into this house.

(Pause.)

Debbie: Do you really like Toronto?

Carolyn: It's okay. It's kind of good and kind of bad. My job is good, very good. I've had two promotions and they all seem to like my work. I work a lot of hours but the money's good.

Debbie: It doesn't sound like much fun to me. But, if you like it, why not?

Carolyn: Right now it's good for me. I don't have many friends, I'm just getting to know people. My apartment's small, so working a lot suits me. Besides, there are some nice guys at work.

Debbie: Finally, a juicy part. Do you date much? Do you see someone regularly?

Carolyn: It's really hard to meet men. I've gone out with several guys. Mostly they're from work, but it never seems to work out. They either come on too strong or I start to like them and *I* come on. It just doesn't seem to work out. (Pause.) It's like I have to win all the time.

Debbie: You're better off than me. I always have to lose.

(Pause.)

Carolyn: I have an idea. Why don't you come to Toronto with me? The apartment's small but I have a hide-a-bed and we could both live there.

Debbie: Oh, Care! (Initial excitement gives way to doubt.) It sounds good, but—

Carolyn: There are jobs there. I could get you one where I work.

Debbie: But I don't know anyone.

Carolyn: You know me.

Debbie: Yes, that's true enough. (Pause.) But I couldn't go. Not just now.

(Pause.)

Carolyn: Is it because of Andy? Do you want to stay here because of him?

Debbie: There's no Andy. Not in my life anyway.

Carolyn: What happened?

Debbie: You won't give up, will you? You're going to keep hounding me until I tell you everything that happened.

Carolyn: Is it as bad as all that?

Debbie: You decide. I'll tell you what you want to know and then you tell me how bad you think it is. (Pause.) After you left, mother got sick. She lost a lot of weight. Oh, don't worry, she's okay now. But she couldn't eat. She couldn't sleep, couldn't keep anything down. Diarrhea, too. Dad was worried sick. But he had to work so I did what had to be done. I stayed with her. Held her hand. Took care of her and the house. She got worse and I stayed home more and more. I did everything. It was incredible, but I did it. I took care of Mom, the house, Dad, everything. Me! Little Debbie who never had a serious thought. I ran the place. (Pause.) I even got to like it. I was needed. Not just a scatter-brain kid. Care, I was someone important.

(Pause.)

Carolyn: And then what happened?

Debbie: Mother got better. It was slow at first. There would be weeks when she would feel good and I'd think it was okay to get out of the house, but whenever I did, when I came home she'd be sick in the bathroom and Dad would be trying to help her and he'd be doing something wrong. You know how helpless he is. So, I just stayed home. After a while, her problems stopped and she started doing things again. (Pause.) Eventually, I didn't have anything to do. She took everything back. (Pause.) It was then that Dad asked me to work for him.

(The conversation stops. Debbie takes a drink and, although she has been drinking since the conversation started, Carolyn takes special notice this time.)

Carolyn: When did the drinking start?

Debbie: What drinking?

Carolyn: Oh oh. It's going to be like that, is it?

Debbie: (mimicing) It's going to be like that, is it?

(Carolyn is shocked. There is silence as Carolyn looks at Debbie and Debbie looks away.)

Debbie: I'm sorry. I just want to avoid lecture number sisteen, er ah sixteen.

(Pause.)

Carolyn: That's okay. (Pause.) What about Andy?

Debbie: He got tired of waiting. He was good for a while but when we started going out again it wasn't the same. I had to hurry home or he had to wait around while I phoned to check on things. I guess he just got tired.

Carolyn: And your other friends?

Debbie: They got tired, too.

Carolyn: It sounds awful. (Pause.) It also sounds like it's a good time to make a change. We could have a lot of fun together. I could show you the city. We could get a bigger apartment and share the rent. Come on, Debbie. Let's do it.

Debbie: It sounds like a lot of fun. You could really help me get a job?

Carolyn: Sure.

Debbie: Oh, Carolyn. I don't know.

Carolyn: There's so much to do there. You could do what you want. Make your own friends. I wouldn't tell you how to run your life.

Debbie: Are you sure I wouldn't be in your way?

Carolyn: Don't be silly. I'm really inviting you.

Debbie: What would I tell Mom and Dad?

Carolyn: Tell them? Tell them the truth. Tell them you're moving out.

Debbie: Just like that?

Carolyn: Yes. Just like that.

Debbie: I couldn't do that. Not on their anniversary.

Carolyn: Okay. Wait till tomorrow. Tell them then. We can still go back together.

Debbie: Maybe I could leave them a note. Better still, will you tell them for me?

Carolyn: No. I'll be with you, if you want, but it is your decision and you have to tell them.

Debbie: But I don't think I could.

Carolyn: It's a perfect time. Tomorrow. It's your chance.

Debbie: Do you mean this is a one-time offer?

Carolyn: What I mean is that you should leave this house and this is a good time.

Debbie: I can't. I can't do it.

Carolyn: (frustrated) You mean you won't. You won't take control of your life. You won't free yourself. Look at you!

(Carolyn picks up the mirror from the table and thrusts it in front of Debbie.)

Carolyn: (continuing) Overweight. Unhappy. Wasting yourself. And you won't do anything about it. I'd like
to shake some sense into you. You're pathetic.

Debbie: Perhaps I am. I just know I'm not like you and
I'm glad of that. Just because you left, just about
killing us, you think that everyone else can do the
same. Well, we're not like you. I can't turn my
back on my family.

Carolyn: Don't you see what's happening?

Debbie: No. There's nothing happening. Go away. Go
back to your big city. Leave me alone.

Carolyn: You can't see what they're doing to you, can you.

Debbie: You're wrong. They need me. I need them. Leave
me alone.

Carolyn: They've really swallowed you. You're the lamb—

(Debbie runs from the kitchen through door right. She is
screaming, virtually in hysterics.)

Debbie: No! No! Stop it!

Carolyn: (continuing)—being slaughtered. And they don't
even have the grace to do it swiftly.

(Carolyn leans against the table. She talks to herself.)

Carolyn: (continuing) Now what? What a mess. (Pause.) A
year ago when I felt like this, I walked out that
door. That one right there, never to return, or so
I thought. And now, here I am again. Feeling
ugly. Feeling like I want to run again. What is
there about this place? What's here that's so wrong?
(Pause.) Brace yourself, here they come.

(Voices can be heard from behind door right. Carolyn backs away from the door. William enters followed by Beverly.)

William: (disdainfully and with unconcealed hostility) Oh. It's you.

Carolyn: Hello, Dad.

Beverly: Carolyn!

Carolyn: Mom.

(Carolyn and Beverly start toward each other but stop when William begins to speak.)

William: We wondered what happened to Debbie. We should have known that you were behind it.

Beverly: And you two were always such good friends.

William: Home how long? Five minutes? Ten minutes? And the place is all upset again.

Carolyn: I didn't plan it this way. It just happened.

William: Is this why you came back? To screw things up? We're just getting over your last departure.

Beverly: Now, William—

William: Don't "now, William" me. That's right. Every time she's around the place is upset. Everything is nice and smooth and then bang, in walks Carolyn and all hell breaks loose.

Carolyn: Honest, Dad. I didn't mean it. Whatever it was that I said, I didn't mean it.

Beverly: You see, Will? She meant well.

Carolyn: There's no one in the world that I want to hurt less than Debbie.

Beverly: That's right. That's how we all feel.

William: NO! It's just the same as it was before. Those are only words. What is it with you? Do you get your kicks from hurting us?

Carolyn: No. It isn't like that.

Beverly: William. Please lower your voice. What if the guests should arrive?

Carolyn: It isn't like that at all.

Beverly: William, please. Debbie invited her. She's a guest. She's come all this way. Let's be nice. We can be angry tomorrow. Let's try to be pleasant tonight. For me? Did you have a nice flight?

(William turns away from Beverly and Carolyn and looks out the window, turning his back on them.)

Carolyn: Yes. Just fine.

Beverly: Are you hungry? Did they feed you on the plane? You look just skin and bones.

Carolyn: I'm okay. I had plenty to eat. How is everything here?

Beverly: Just fine. It's just the same. I'm busy here and Dad is working hard. Debbie helps him, did you know?

Carolyn: She told me that she'd been doing a lot. That you were sick. I'm sorry to hear that.

William: (without turning around) You should be.

Beverly: I'm all right now. I just have this cough every now and then.

Carolyn: Can't doctors help?

Beverly: They can't seem to find anything. They say it's all in my head. It's getting better, though, all the time. Isn't it, William?

William: (agreeing) mmm . . .

(Pause.)

Beverly: Your room is all ready for you. Where's your suitcase?

Carolyn: It's downtown. At a hotel.

Beverly: At a hotel? You're not staying with us?

William: Good.

Carolyn: I didn't know how it would be here. I didn't know how well it would go. I got a room, just in case.

Beverly: That makes me feel really bad. This is terrible. You, our own daughter, not even feeling like you could stay here.

Carolyn: Well, when I left, the situation was strained.

William: It got lots worse, too.

Beverly: You'll just have to change your mind and stay here. At least for tonight. William, tell her it's all right. Will you?

William: I really don't care. She can stay here, or downtown, or in Timbuktu. I couldn't care less.

Beverly: See? Your father says it's all right.

(Pause. The matter is left unresolved.)

Carolyn: I was surprised to see how Debbie looked.

Beverly: Hasn't she grown up? She was such a help when
           I was sick. She took care of everything.

Carolyn: She told me. It's too bad that she quit university.

Beverly: She'll go back sometime. She's helping her dad
           now. That's important, isn't it, Will.

William: (still not turning around and with a touch of irony)
           I don't know what I'd do without her.

Carolyn: It's going to be very hard for her to get a good
           job without some kind of degree or training. To
           make something of herself.

Beverly: But she has a job. A good one, too. Right, William?

Carolyn: Do you mean that it's permanent?

Beverly: For as long as she wants it. Isn't that right, William?

(William whirls around and glares at Carolyn.)

William: What did you and Debbie talk about?

Carolyn: What? About what happened when I was gone.
           About what she's doing and what she'd like to do.

William: And what did *you* say about what she'd like to do?

Carolyn: I won't lie. I told her she should get out of this
           house. That she should do something with her life.

William: That she should be like you?

Carolyn: No. That she should be herself. Save herself. That
           she should leave this place and come and live with
           me.

(Beverly gets very agitated. She starts to breathe erratically.)

Beverly: Oh, no.

William: (to Beverly) Are you all right? (calls) Debbie! Debbie!

Beverly: (waves her hand without looking at him) I'm all right. Don't bother Debbie. (They sit quietly.) Can't you talk about it tomorrow?

William: Yes. We'll talk about it later.

Carolyn: No. Tomorrow will be too late. Now's the time. Now, when we're angry. We won't be so honest tomorrow.

William: So what's so important that it can't wait.

Carolyn: Debbie is that important.

Beverly: She's very important. Very young.

Carolyn: (to William) Don't you see what is happening to Debbie? She is overweight, unkempt, miserable, and, unless I miss my guess, virtually an alcoholic. Can't you see she's a disaster.

William: It's not my fault. I tried to help her. I gave her something to do. Do you think I want her there at the store? Just sitting around all day?

Carolyn: If you really wanted to help her, you'd help her go back to school. Help her do something else. Help her leave.

Beverly: We want whatever is best for her.

William: (over Beverly) I'll help *you*, though. I'll help you leave. Who do you think you are? What makes you think you can just pop in here out of the blue and tell us how we should act. We went through some real shit this past year, and we came through okay. No thanks to you. Now you think you can come back and tell us how to do things.

Beverly: That's right. We know Debbie best of all.

William: It isn't up to you to tell any of us how to live. And that includes Debbie. You think its your job. Well, Miss Busybody, I'll tell you right now that it isn't.

Carolyn: It's not my job, I agree. (to William) It's yours and you're the only one around here who can do it. You, of all people, should understand. You know what it's like to be trapped.

William: I don't know what you're talking about.

Carolyn: Do you really think I don't know? You might be able to fool some people, your friends, maybe, and even Debbie. But we know, you and I, we know. You told me a lot and I figured out the rest.

Beverly: What is she talking about, William?

William: Nothing. Nothing at all. (to Carolyn) You had better go. Now.

Carolyn: I'll go all right. Don't worry. But I'm going to tell you something about what it's like to be a part of this family. Maybe then you'll understand Debbie a little better.

(William threatens Carolyn.)

Beverly: Wait, William. She's going to tell us what she's been doing.

(William throws up his hands in futility.)

Carolyn: It started way back when I was a child and you kept me at home. I was Mother's little helper. Help Mother with this. Help Mother with that. Be Daddy's big girl. Take care of Debbie. Never once was I allowed to be myself. I couldn't be an ordinary kid. I couldn't play outside or take my chances.

Beverly: But each time you went out you got frightened. You begged me to keep you in, to protect you. You wanted to be protected from the "dark places," as you called them. You were so frail. I'll get a picture of you. You'll see. (She starts to get up.)

Carolyn: Never mind, Mother. (to William) You know what I'm saying.

William: (uncertainly) Go on.

Carolyn: Childhood was just the beginning and when I got older, the situation was worse. My friends had to be approved. I didn't even date until I was eighteen and out of high school.

William: You're not blaming us for that, are you?

Beverly: You know we wanted you to date. Remember the time that nice boy from church asked you out and you thought you didn't want to go? We made you go out with him. Remember?

Carolyn: (to William) Sometime I decided that I had to esca— er, leave, in order to be myself. But I was nothing. I couldn't even talk to anyone without blushing. I couldn't support myself. I decided to stay here and put up with it until I could get out. I counted the days. I even counted the hours.

William: What's this got to do with anything?

Carolyn: It's what I had to put up with and when I left, the same thing happened to Debbie. And now look at her. You know it's true. You know that first me and then Debbie have made this family possible. Your deal with Mother, her money for your care, is so sick that it has resulted in this.

William: Do you have any idea what it is you're saying?

Carolyn: Of course I do. I'm saying that years ago this marriage was just about finished. I believe you were interested in Marge Simpson at the time. She was healthy and attractive but she didn't have any money. So you stayed married and took care of Mother and used the money that she inherited when Grandpa died. But your marriage was still sour and Debbie and I became the sweeteners. We helped take care of Mother. We helped keep you content. You both used us rather than fix up your own lives. You know that what I'm saying is true. (Pause.) Listen to your feelings. What do they say? Look around, what do you see?

Beverly: I think it's a very nice kitchen.

William: I think you've said quite enough now.

Carolyn: There's just one more thing. Remember how angry you got last year?

William: And I should have been. The way you used us. You pretended to love us and you lived here and went to university.

(Beverly tries to interrupt here and at a few later points. She does not succeed.)

William: (continuing) You pretended to love us while all the time you knew that as soon as you got your chance you'd be long gone.

Carolyn: That's how little you understand. I worked my head off to be free. To get an education so that I could get out of here. And then you planned that stupid graduation party for me. You didn't even ask if I wanted one. That was it. Graduating was my victory. For me. Alone. I couldn't let you take that away.

(Pause.)

Carolyn: (continuing) Do you understand what I'm saying?

William: I'm not stupid. I do manage to understand some things. I understand that what I call "marriage" you call a "deal." What I call "loyalty," you call "sickness." What I call "being used," you call a "victory."

Carolyn: Can you be loyal to more than just Mother? Can you be loyal to Debbie? Help Debbie out?

William: (looking at Beverly) My first responsibility is to her. My first care, my first loyalty. My first devotion. (Pause.) Husband first and father second.

(Pause.)

Carolyn: I guess that's it, then.

William: Yes. There's nothing more to say. The decision was made a long time ago and now we see it through.

Carolyn: No matter who gets hurt.

William: No matter. Life is full of compromises.

(Pause.)

Beverly: No more argument?

Carolyn: No, Mom. No more. We're done.

Beverly: I'm so glad. This is wonderful. Perfect. Peace at last. What an anniversary.

(The doorbell rings. William and Beverly look at each other. They smile.)

William: The guests have arrived, my dear, for our silver wedding anniversary.

(The bell rings again.)

Debbie: (off camera) I'll get it.

Beverly: Our Debbie is such a big help.

William: Well, Mother, shall we celebrate? (He offers her his arm.) We've earned it.

(William and Beverly head toward door right and they stop when they get to it. They turn and look at Carolyn.)

William: We'd like you to join us.

Beverly: You can stay as long as you like. Your room is just like you left it.

(They exit and the door is left ajar.)

(Carolyn is alone. The doorbell rings again and sounds of the party begin to come into the kitchen. Carolyn walks to the cupboard and gets a glass. She finds the liquor, pours herself a drink and walks back to the right door and listens to the party sounds. She begins to go through but stops and, instead, she closes the door. She walks to the left door and considers it and then walks back to the center of the kitchen. She looks at the right door and speaks as if to herself.)

ENDING A

Carolyn: A few steps that way and into open arms. The prodigal returns. And on their anniversary—a nice touch. And why not? I could help Debbie. And they want me to. They love me. They need me. Ha! That's a laugh. They don't need me at all. Not even Debbie. They do just fine. They have the world in this house. I'd only spoil it for them. (Pause.) It's a funny feeling, this feeling that it's time to go. Sometimes it hits me. Not just here but other places, too. Even if I'm having a good time. I feel like I've done all that I can, that what I have to give has all been given. That it's time to go.

(She drinks.)

Carolyn: (continuing) There's nothing for me here. There's nothing here for me to do. It's all over now. I have my life. I have to go.

(She exits through door left.)

(FADE OUT)

THE END.

ENDING B

Carolyn: Through that door and into open arms. Through the other and its into the cold again. Back to loneliness. If I leave now I can never return; this part of my life, the family part, will be gone forever. I went out that door last time and it was bad for them. And what did I get? Singles bars and paranoia. Some deal, right? Oh, why did I come back, anyway? To finish things? To see how everyone was doing? Face it, Carolyn, you came back to make *amends*, to be forgiven, to be a part of something again. I must try again to make things right. I love them and I want to help. My life is here, I have to stay.

(She exits through door right.)

(FADE OUT)

THE END.

That is a brief look at the Spencers, a family with a few problems and, of course, some strengths. We will later consider the Spencers in greater detail when they will be used to exemplify ideas related to family interaction; but now, it might be helpful to consider them more informally. Do you know people who are like members of the Spencer family? Which one of the Spencers did you like the most? The least? What is there that you liked or disliked about them? Who was in your opinion the strongest? The weakest? The most in need? What adjective best describes William? Debbie? Beverly? Carolyn? Is there a victim? Is there a victimizer? If they are all trapped, what is preventing them from getting out of the trap?

Do you know families that are like the Spencers? How are these families like the Spencers? What are the commonalities? What differences exist? How does the behavior of each Spencer fit with the behavior of the other members? Consider the adjectives that you applied to each member in the previous paragraph. How does the adjective that you applied to William match with the adjective that you applied to Beverly? And so forth.

It may be that your answers to the above questions indicate that the Spencers as individuals are neither very strong nor very capable. If that is the case, to what do you attribute their success? Apparently, they have friends, money, and a high standing in the community. How can this be, given their shortcomings as family members?

It may be that the answer to this puzzle is to be found in the family's interactions. In short, their personal incompetencies fit together in such a way that the group as a group is successful. (Inheriting a large sum of money helped, of course.) As an example, William's hard work, and his overbearing and aggressive nature help him succeed in business, and these characteristics are made possible by Beverly and Debbie's support and submissiveness at home. On the one hand, his behavior can be seen as tyrannical; at the same time, he protects them. They also protect him.

This protectiveness, of course, has its costs. The major cost is that neither William nor Beverly nor Debbie can function fully as adult persons. This incapacity is not a problem as long as nothing upsets the family's way, as long as they stay within their small world of business and home and control all incoming information. Since maintaining this narrow circumscription is impossible, the Spencers are insecure. In some sense they understand the precariousness of their position and this understanding is the source of their anxiety, their rigidity, and their rejection of ideas that do not fit with their conceptions.

Consider Carolyn's dilemma: to leave or stay. In terms of this book, her dilemma concerns the way her next steps will affect the family system which desperately needs help and how her next steps will affect her life, her personal system. Her dilemma will be resolved on the basis of the way that she perceives herself, her family, and her chances for success in meeting her personal needs.

We have given you a chance to supply the ending which, for you, best fits the play. Which ending do you think makes more sense, given the information about Carolyn and her family which you have gathered from the entire sketch? Which ending do you think makes more sense, given your view of family interaction in general? Which ending makes more sense, given your view on the way people act?

But there are other questions that are raised by these two endings. Some of these questions have to do with what you think Carolyn "ought" to do and some of these questions refer to what you think will happen next.

First, let's consider what Carolyn ought to do. These are not theoretical questions but moral questions. How much should a daughter sacrifice herself for her family? For her parents? For her sister? Is her first responsibility to take care of herself? How will her needs best be met? By making a place for herself in the world and putting up with the pain that attends independence? Or, will her needs best be met by making a place (or by moving into a place already prepared) at home, being part of a family, and putting up with the pain of others' psychological dysfunction? What do you think? Your answers can give you some information about your ideas regarding family and personal responsibility.

The last set of questions concerns what will happen next. If Carolyn stays, what do you think the chances will be that her sister will change? Why do you think her sister does not want her to stay? Will Carolyn be able to help Debbie since Debbie wants her to go? How will her staying affect the way the family system works? Will her staying help her mother become more active? More competent? Will the system take Carolyn in? How will that absorption occur? Will the system include her no matter how she acts? Or, will the family include her only on condition that she act in certain ways?

The sketch, then, can be used advantageously in several ways. It can be used to explore our thoughts about families, these thoughts that affect the way we see family life. The sketch can be used to help us explore the way that family systems work. Finally, the sketch will be used throughout the remainder of our book as a source of examples.

Chapter 3

UNDERSTANDING THE FAMILY

A Synthesis of Systems and
Other Ideas

Thus far, we have provided the background for our inquiring into family life from the standpoint of systems theory. This background has included information about our approach and what we hope to accomplish, information about the principles that will direct our inquiry, and information about problems with using "cause" in reference to social interaction. These are important preliminaries and what now follows is the substance of our inquiry.

A family is a system and has properties characteristic of systems in general. Moreover, a family is a living system and has properties that it shares with other mindful systems, these properties being different from those of physical science systems. Still more specifically, the family is a unique type of living system, the uniqueness having its origins in the reasons for which it was established and the resulting organization. To explore the family as a system, we will begin with some definitions and then show the ways in which the family is like other systems, and those in which it is a special case.

A system is usually defined as a collection of interrelated parts and the existing relationships among the parts. All systems are alike in this regard; their parts are interconnected and form a whole. Also, systems are alike in that limits to membership exist. That is, a system's parts can be identified in some way and the parts of systems can be differentiated from external elements. Transactions occur between some of the system's parts and these external elements. Systems have some force which holds them together and, at the same time, there are tendencies toward disintegration. These are the characteristics of all systems, whether they are physical systems or biological ones.

Although systems have common characteristics, physical science systems (systems associated with physics, chemistry, electricity, hydraulics, and thermodynamics) are different from biological systems (such as persons, families, trees). The difference is to be found in the ability of biological systems to adapt to *information*. The form of any living system is the result of its personally unique and species-specific *attempt to adapt*.

As Bateson put it, the form of any living thing or group is the result of its transformation of information into its structure (Bateson, 1979). That is, the shape, form, structure of any living thing (or collection of living things) is the result of the way that the living thing[17] has *changed itself in order to survive*, given its *interpretation of the genetic and contextual information* it has received.

For example, a tree receives information about the supply of water and the source of light, and the tree's form (its height, the shape, size, and number of leaves, its root system, etc.) is the result of the way it has adapted to such contextual information given its genetic endowment. Some of the transformations of information occur within the life of a species member (stunted trees at high elevations) and others are the result of evolutionary process (modern trees being different from trees of a million years ago).

The important point about all this, however, is that trees and other living systems adapt to their context (change their structure) but physical systems do not.[15]

So, a living system or its parts can take in information, assign some meaning to this information and, at some level and in a way which reflects its existing structure, modify itself in order to live in the changed situation as it has defined it. Families do this. A family begins when two people begin to relate to each other in a particular (intimate) way. The couple's unique way is a mix of personal characteristics that occurs in a particular social context. That is, individual competencies, needs, and behavior are combined in a singular way and the combination follows cultural prescriptions as these prescriptions are defined by the two persons. The cultural prescriptions are "information," and the couple's structure of relationship reflects this information. With the passage of time, different information is received as the persons age, as (and if) they have children, and as their social and geographical and economic situation changes. Their survival as a family requires that they adapt to these changes and the kind of accommodation that the family makes is determined (Maturana, 1978; Dell, 1985) by its structure. That is, *adaptation depends on a family's established interaction and transaction patterns, rather than being dependent on raw information that its members receive.*

Consider the Spencers as a living system. The structure of the Spencer family is greatly affected by the characteristics of human beings as a species. There are two generations of Spencers because the dependency of young human beings creates families of two or more generations. The older generation contains a Mr. Spencer and a Mrs. Spencer because the fact that the creation of new life requires two cross-sex people (not one or three) promotes the creation of families with two adults, one of each sex. The Spencer family lives in a house and each attempts to help the other because the psychological and physical fraility of humans promotes the creation of families that are supportive, safe, and which provide adequate shelter from the elements. So, the Spencers are like many other human families the world round because humans as a species receive genetic information that is transformed into a particular organization we call family.

But North American families are organized in a different fashion from other families in other lands. The form of

North American families is different from the form of families elsewhere because the information received is different. Information regarding appropriate roles, interaction, levels of democracy, authoritarianism, freedom, and responsibility is culturally specific and the families in any particular cultural context have a similar organization because of the information to which the families are exposed. The Spencers work hard, and work together, and forsake all others as these, among other bits of information, are cultural expectations which affect their family organization.

The structure of the Spencer family, like the structure of every other family, developed slowly over time and the structure not only reflected the interpretation of information (as we have seen) but the structure determined how information would be interpreted (which we will now briefly consider). Let us now investigate how the Spencers' structure determines the way that information is interpreted, how the structure works to limit the Spencers' successful interpretation of information.

Carolyn brought information to the Spencer family system and the family's structure specified how that information was to be received. The information could not enter the system through Debbie nor could it enter through Mrs. Spencer; the structure did not allow either person to carry information into the system. The only way the information could enter the system was through Mr. Spencer and he was strong enough to blunt its effect. The Spencers' structure was such that Debbie had to say, "Don't talk to *me* about it, tell *them*." Mrs. Spencer's symptomatic behavior said, "Don't tell me, tell your father." Mr. Spencer said, "Forget it, you're crazy." In this way the family's structure allowed each Spencer to continue acting as they had been acting—without having to deal with Carolyn's interpretation of their situation.

Most observers would say that the Spencer family does not work very well, and this could be traced to the way they uniquely interpreted information and idiosyncratically acted on that interpretation to build a structure. This structure then, affected subsequent interpretation of information and the resulting misinterpretation confounded their difficulties as poor structure and misinterpretation proceeded hand in hand.

A family can be classified as a system and it has properties that are characteristic of systems in general. Moreover, a family is a unique system which is organized in a particular way. This uniqueness gives it special characteristics which other systems do not have. To explore the family as a system, we will begin with two definitions and then proceed to show how a family is like all other systems and, also, how it is a special case.

DEFINITION OF A FAMILY SYSTEM

A system is generally defined as a collection of interrelated components and the existing relationships among the components. A family system would be the collection of people whose behavior is interrelated in a particular way and the relationships that exist among these people. Clarity demands that "in a particular way" be explained. For a group to be classified as a family, as "family" is considered here, it must be legally, or socially, or internally defined as a family and its interaction must have certain characteristics. The characteristics of family-type interaction result from the members' attempts to fulfill the family's major social functions. In contemporary North America, the major function is the fulfillment of the members' needs for intimacy.[19]

It is the meeting of intimacy needs that contributes most to the uniqueness of family interaction. Intimacy requires a relationship of length; it is associated with a person's being "known," with being seen as a whole person and not just as a player of some role. Intimacy also includes the surrender of self without a sense of loss or "being taken." Not all families achieve intimacy at high levels and the level of intimacy in any family varies over time. Nevertheless, it is the fact that people handle their intimacy needs in the family setting that gives family-type interaction its special characteristics.

The "nuclear family" of contemporary society with its once married mother and father and their dependent children fits into the family category because: (1) it is legally recognized as a family, (2) it is generally recognized in our society as an acceptable family form, (3) the members see themselves as a family, (4) it meets (or seems to meet) members' intimacy needs and it fulfills the other functions prescribed by society, and (5) it is life-long or at least the members expect permanence.

Other groups, such as unmarried cohabiting couples, gay couples, childless (child-free) couples, blended families, and single-parent families are less commonly categorized as families because they lack at least one of the listed characteristics. Cohabiting couples have an uncertain legal status as do gay couples. Gay couples are not generally recognized as a family. Childless and gay couples do not fulfill the procreation function that is a social expectation. Blended and single parent families are usually the result of impermanence.

In this book, we take the broad view; we see all of the above as families. These family types may be structurally different from nuclear families and they may not always be seen as families by the public at large but, nevertheless, we believe they are families and subject to family systems analysis. For our purposes, they are families because in solving problems associated with integration, pattern effectiveness, and intimacy, they generate interaction patterns and adopt structural strategies that are typical of families whether they be nuclear or not. Moreover, inasmuch as fewer than half of the families in North America are standard nuclear families, the elimination of these other forms would be unrealistic.

Therefore, *a family is a family if it does what families do.* As we have said, the most important contribution that a family makes to the lives of its members is to provide a context of intimacy. If a group comes together for that purpose, in our book, it is a family.

As a system, each family has characteristics which it shares with other living systems. In the following, we specify the characteristics of family systems and other mindful systems.

CHARACTERISTICS OF SYSTEMS

Our consideration of systems and family systems will proceed in a series of steps as we move from simple ideas toward more complex analyses. Generally, our approach will be first to present an idea and then to show how this idea helps us to understand families.

The Arbitrary Nature of Systems Analysis

That which is called a system is the product of an arbitrary sectioning of the universe. We talk of systems as though there were many, but there is only one system with many subsystems. A hierarchy of systems exists. A system's size is directly related both to its complexity and the difficulty associated with analyzing it. We have neither the skills nor the tools to analyze systems that are very complicated. Therefore, we break a system into parts and think about the parts as though they were systems.

Clear thinking is advanced by remembering that what we term "system" results from our arbitrary division of the real and total universe. That which we call a system would be called a subsystem if we broadened our view to include another level (Koestler, 1978). Even though we remove a subsystem from its context and call it a system, this removal is only in our analysis; the subsystem that we have objectified (that which we now call a system) will continue to fit into the larger system of which it is a part. We call a family a system and it is composed of subsystems (persons, coalitions); families also are subsystems if we consider them as components of the social system. Our making families into systems was an arbitrary choice which was based on our desire to study family life.

The way that systems fit together is important to understanding social life. The importance of this fit is illustrated by a consideration of the divorce rate. In attempting to understand the increased divorce rate, some people concentrate on the family unit and see the "problem" as having its source in the family. Some see the increased divorce rate as having its source in individualism, and others see the problem as reflecting larger social issues. Each of these perspectives analyzes the issue from a too-narrow perspective and misses the systems idea that individuals, families, and the larger society are all interconnected. That is, the systems theory explanation of the high divorce rate is that it reflects the mix of non-family social realities (disorganization, rapid change, pluralism, economic inbalance and uncertainty), non-family individual realities (high levels of anxiety and frustration, an emphasis on personal growth, economic non-dependence, longer lives), and family realities (insularity, separation from kin, emotional intensity, demand-capability imbalance).

The systems view holds that all systems are connected and that no system operates without being influenced by some other system. When we arbitrarily separate one system from the others we may improve our perception of the internal workings of the separated system but, at the same time, we lose sight of the way these inner workings reflect the system's context, the other systems with which it transacts. A full view requires that we look at systems "from both sides now"; but this simultaneous all-encompassing view, unfortunately, is virtually impossible. We can, however, recognize our problem and be sensitive to the possible effect of transactional influences when we focus on interaction.

Continuous Interaction

It is a characteristic of systems that interaction is continuous, of a piece with former patterns. All interaction has precedents and the actors' behaviors are always mutually contingent. That is, one actor's behavior is inextricably intertwined with the past and present behavior of himself and the other actors.

The idea of continuing and mutually involved interaction can be a difficult one to grasp. The difficulty is to be found in the fact that language (Bateson, 1979) and perception tend to encourage us to objectify things and people and promote our seeing ourselves as separate entities. However, to see human behavior as interactional, we must change our epistemology so that we no longer separate ourselves from those others with whom we interact. The new epistemology suggests that we take responsibility not only for what we do but also for that with which we are involved. When people are seen as mutually involved, interaction is a very complicated matter;

there is complexity where we wish for simplicity. But, whether we like it or not, the complexity must be considered if we are to better understand our action and our interaction.

Each of us tends to make sense out of the complexity of continuing interaction by "punctuating" (Watzlawick et al., 1967) this interaction in a particular way. Just as the flow of words on this page has punctuation marks and paragraphs which allow (we hope) readers to make some sense of the words, each of us reconstructs interaction sequences by "punctuating," by dividing the continuous flow of action into non-continuous segments. That is, we arbitrarily construct a sequence with a beginning and an end. Anyone who has ever tried to sort out an interaction problem of the type, " 'He started it'—'But he hit me first' " has experienced the difficulties that attend the disparate punctuation of continuous interaction.

Consider how the Spencers punctuated events. Carolyn punctuated her previous leaving as though it was a reasonable reaction to the way she had been treated. Mr. Spencer saw her leaving as a betrayal of the family and he saw Carolyn as the family villain. Both Carolyn and Mr. Spencer are commenting on the same event but their punctuation, being based on their self-serving perceptions, is decidedly different.

Such punctuation and the self-serving positing of cause and effect is contrary to ideas of the mutuality and interinvolvement of system components. Nevertheless, punctuation allows us to make some sense out of what is happening to us and around us. It is unfortunate that "making sense" is afforded by a distortion of reality.

Integration

Even the most casual and superficial consideration of systems acknowledges that the parts of some systems stay together over time but, in other systems, the components break apart and go their separate ways. The term "integration" refers to the system's unity, and its opposite is "disintegration."[20] Although all systems have some trouble with maintaining their level of integration, the disintegration of family systems receives the most attention. In a later part of the book,[21] we consider family integration; in the next few paragraphs our aim is to indicate that a family's integration is not something that can be taken for granted.

Families are fragile units (this is another way of saying that integration is problematic) for a number of reasons. First, unlike an arm which cannot exist if separated from the body, members can leave the family and still exist and sometimes they do exactly that. In today's world of dissolvable families, a family's continued unity requires that members pay attention to the needs of others so that, having their needs met, the others will maintain their family membership.

Also, families are fragile because we expect much of family members and these members are ill-prepared to meet the high expectations. We expect that family members will love and be loved and that their intimacy needs will be met. We expect that socialization of the young will occur, that families will provide stability and that families will absorb the anxiety and frustration that are created elsewhere in contemporary life. We expect that conjugal sexual activity will be always exciting and innovative, that members will be nurtured, and housed, clothed, and fed properly. These expectations are difficult to meet and they would be unrealistic even if supports were available. The unhappy truth is that contemporary families are frequently left alone without support from either kin or social institutions. Finding ways to fulfill expectations and thereby maintain integration is a problem which every family must solve.

Family integration is maintained in several ways. As noted, family integration is supported if the members' needs are met. Some of these needs are basic (food, shelter, clothing) and other needs, although not quite "basic," are very nearly as important (intimacy, esteem, social contact, and sex). Both kinds of needs are met in families and members will tend to support those family environments in which these needs are met.

Families also maintain their unity because family life becomes habitual, because we fear the unknown, and because we are uncomfortable with taking risks. We tend to live with what we have rather than destroy it and attempt to find some more satisfying relationship. There is never any guarantee that a new and superior relationship will develop that will compensate for the pain and difficulty that always attends dissolution. With no such guarantee, we tend to stand pat.

Lastly, society encourages the integration of families. Until the second half of the twentieth century, society *required* that families stay together and family "breakdown" was seen as a sign of personal failure. Although the situation is now different, residues of the thinking that "separation means failure" remain. If separation means failure, integration signifies success. Family integration is encouraged by the culture's relating self-esteem with success and success with the duration of relationship.

Of course, integration has a positive side as well. Families maintain their integration because people *enjoy* what is happening there. Members develop a family identity, a sense of self, and a way of life. Babies are born, and houses are built, and other tasks are begun which members *wish to see through* to conclusion. We share experiences with other family members and, whether good or bad, these experiences *interest* us and our shared interest ties us one to the other. We establish roles that fit together in a particular way and we become comfortable with the fit. We come to know other family members and we can predict how they will respond; we find this predictability reassuring.[22]

The ties that integrate families can either be supportive of personal growth and family harmony or can be detrimental to either. Some families, and the Spencers are a good example, have members who fit together because they support each others' unhealthy characteristics. The Spencers, for example, stay together and interaction is characterized by Mr. Spencer's vacillation between support and reproof of both his daughter Debbie and his wife, Mrs. Spencer's attempt to control through dependence, and Debbie's "sacrifices." Carolyn also helps support the family's continued integration by serving as the reprobate, someone who will come when called and stir things up when the others begin to forget how they are "supposed" to act. It seems that, frequently, *a family's interactions reflect the state of health of the least well member.* When there are several members who function poorly as individuals, family interaction is likely to reflect and augment this poor functioning.

On the other side, families can be integrated through the combination of members' strengths. Support can be given when it is needed in such a way that dependence does not result, roles can mesh both harmoniously and productively, thoughts can be expressed clearly and honestly, joy can abound. Families that are united by such a union of needs, values, and actions are indeed both strong and fortunate.

Transactional Differentiation

Systems, as indicated above, can be classified as subsystems inasmuch as they are parts of larger systems. Each part can be differentiated from the larger system and can be differentiated from other elements at the same level. For example, a family is part of a social system, but can be differentiated from that larger social system and from other families. "Differentiated" does not mean "separate," "differentiated" means only that the family is a recognizable component of the larger social system. In the same way, each family member is recognizable as a differentiated and unique part of the family.

We will refer to a system member's dealing with nonsystem elements as "transactions" and we will refer to intrasystemic activity as "interaction." A family member transacts with schoolmates or business associates, and family members interact with each other.

A family, because it is differentiated from other families and other parts of the social system, is an identifiable unit. The Spencers are an identifiable group with a known membership. Each Spencer has had dealings with elements of the larger system (school, church, work, other families) and these elements are not part of the Spencer family. These nondomestic dealings are the Spencer's transactions. When the Spencers are in their house in the evening and no outsiders are present, the Spencers are interacting. Both ideas, interaction and transaction, require the family's differentiation from its context.[23]

Levels of Systems and Their Properties

System levels.   First, we will consider the levels of family systems and then we will think about the properties of different levels.   Since a system is defined as an interrelated set of components and the relationship among these components, it is obvious that a system has parts.   These parts are of the system; they are subsystems.

There are three levels within the family system: the family, coalitions of members, and individual family members.   In this section, our major concern is to specify a system's (a family's) properties as these contrast with a subsystem's (a member's) properties.   In a subsequent section, we will be concerned with the properties of coalitions.

That the family and its members are at different logical levels is indicated by the fact that what is "good" for the family is not necessarily "good" for the members as individuals. In systems that are functioning well, the well-being of both the system and the subsystem components is simultaneously advanced (Hampden-Turner, 1981).   This is an enviable condition but one which frequently is missing in families.   More often, family well-being runs counter to the short-run well-being of at least one member.

Another indication of the existence of different system levels is the fact that a family member can leave a family system and both will change but both can survive.   Since families are able to survive when members leave and the members are able to survive as well, the existence of two levels, family and person, is obvious.

The final point regarding the existence of levels has to do with internal processes of maturation.   Personal development is somewhat independent of the development of others. "Somewhat" is used because a person's developmental progress *is* influenced by interactional factors; persons do not mature in a vacuum.   However, development, especially maturational development, is generally a matter of a person's internal processes and occurs whether anyone likes it or not. Personal development occurs in the family and affects interaction but it does not originate at the family level; it is a person's *property*.

The properties of levels.   As we have previously indicated, a family has different properties than has its members. Family members can think and feel; a family cannot. "I feel sad" makes sense; "the family feels sad" is incomprehensible. A relationship can be intimate but a person cannot. "We are close" can be understood; "I am close" makes no sense. The way that family characteristics differ from those of members of families will now be considered in detail.

First, to illustrate a way of looking at properties, we will consider goals and specify if goals are an individual's or a family's attribute. The consideration of goals brings to light difficulties with the idea of "consensus" and these difficulties are considered. Then we will explore the idea of emergence.

First of all, we believe that a goal is an idea, an idea that something has value, and this something of value is worth more than alternatives. Inasmuch as a goal is an idea, it is a person's property: only persons have the wherewithal to have ideas.

Consider the matter of "family goal" or, more correctly, "family's goal."[24] Clearly, a family can only have goals which are the goals held by family members. It is nonsense to suggest, for example, that a family has a goal of home ownership when all family members wish to live in an apartment. Similarly, it is not helpful to think of a family as having particular goals if not all of the members have these goals. What would it mean if we were to say that a family has a goal of high educational achievement if it is only the parents who have the goal? In situations of these two types, it is clear that goals must be attributed to persons and not to families.

The problem of goals becomes more difficult when there appears to be a consensus among family members, and all members are agreed that they will attempt to achieve some particular end. In a sense, if family members agree on a goal and they work together to reach it, the individuals' goals become a collective "family's goal." So, the addition of family consensus and purposive interaction to "family's goal" helps to solve the problem because "family's goal" means that, in addition to an idea held in common, there is sharing (the reaching of consensus) and concerted effort to reach that goal. It is both the sharing and the interaction that adds the family dimension to thought, an individual's property.

Let us say that two peole get together for the reason that each wants to get rich. Each has a personal goal but the goal of "getting rich" is never discussed. There is, then, no family's goal. (Few would think that a husband and wife who hold the same goal but who neither share it nor work in harmony to reach it have a "family's goal.") When the husband and wife discuss each one's goal of great wealth, when they agree that gaining wealth is a mutually held goal, and when they work together to make lots of money, there can be said to exist a family's goal. We believe then, that a family's goal can be said to exist if it is understood that the family part of "family's goal" consists of the processes of agreeing on a goal and the subsequent interaction to attain the goal.

Consensus and working agreement. In the preceding paragraphs, we have used the word "consensus," because it is commonly used to describe some sort of agreement among family members. Usually, when the word consensus is used, ideas of democratic process are engendered; we think of the family members quietly sitting down together and discussing some weighty matter and arriving at an agreement that will be mutually satisfactory, equally well understood, and one that will be harmoniously and simultaneously advanced by all the family members. This is, of course, not the way that events usually occur in the world of families. Since "consensus" indicates an unreal state of affairs, we find the term unusable.

What is wrong with "consensus" is that it is not specific enough. The word does not indicate how the decision is made, nor does it indicate who makes it. Decisions in a family can be made by one adult without even conferring with other family members, or they can be made by two adults without the children's involvement. Or they can be made by the entire family. In any case, the agreement is still called "consensus."

In addition, once there is "consensus," the idea seems to be that all the family members work in unison and in harmony to see to it that what has been agreed upon is put into practice. Members all work together with the same commitment and with the same understanding of what was agreed upon.

We believe, and we are not alone (Walker, 1985), that it is incorrect to use a term which confuses so many different issues of process, member involvement, and implementation. We suggest another term, family "working agreement" (Montgomery, 1985). A family's working agreement is an understanding that a particular decision or accord or fiat will be the one which, for the time being, will direct the members' activities. Working agreement implies nothing about the way that the decision, accord, or fiat was reached, nor does it specify whether all family members or only one was involved. Process and membership elements are thereby left open to be investigated.

Moreover, the agreement part of "working agreement" does not refer to the decision that was made; it indicates the family members' agreement to abide by the decision. Or, more accurately "agreement" indicates that the family members have agreed to abide by the decision as they understand it. Even more accurately, "agreement" indicates that family members have agreed to abide by (and implement) the decision as they understand it, given their commitment to the ideas in the decision and their commitment to the family. There is ample evidence that no two people will understand a situation in exactly the same way and our experience indicates that in implementing decisions, the spirit is much more willing than the flesh.

We need an expression that will allow us to think about the kinds of family processes that are covered up with "consensus." We nominate "working agreement," since it allows us to explore the process by which the decision, accord, or fiat was reached, the members who were involved in the decision making, the divergent views regarding the decision, and the differences in the levels of commitment to implement what was decided.

A good example of a working agreement can be found in *Silver Anniversary*. According to Carolyn, Mrs. Spencer inherited money which she let Mr. Spencer have to buy "the business." For this, he agreed to take care of her. Between then and the present, Mrs. Spencer has become more and more dependent upon him to provide her with money, to make decisions, and to protect her from the real world. Despite this increased dependency which was probably unanticipated by him, although it may have been anticipated by her, Mr. Spencer has done what he said he would do. Theirs was a working agreement and it set the basis for the family's inter-action patterns over the years. As we can see, not all the family members were involved in the decision making. In fact, no explicit decision may have been made at all—the decision may just have evolved. Not all the family members saw the decision the same way nor were equally committed to it.

Of course, some working agreements are more demo-cratically arrived at than this one and some enhance growth to a greater extent. Some are more generally agreeable and some are better implemented. Some working agreements *work* better than others to advance family functioning and personal development. Nevertheless, this is a working agreement and should be seen as such.

Emergence. Any thorough consideration of levels and properties must include "emergence." The family has prop-erties not found in its components for the reason that the family is more than a noninteracting heap of individuals. A family consists of persons in interaction and this interaction gives rise to the emergence of that which we call "family." "Emergence" points to the growth of something extra, some property of the whole which cannot be found either in the components or in the simple summation of the characteristics of the components. "Family" is that which is present in interaction but which cannot be found in any member taken separately.

Such phenomena as intimacy, conflict, caring, arguing, and harmony are the properties of families inasmuch as these characteristics cannot be found in persons. These emergent qualities are *derived* from member's attributes, but the qualities that emerge are the product of interaction and cannot be found in the parts taken separately. For example, if an observer were to study conflict in a particular marriage, he would proceed most efficiently by observing the parties in conflict rather than by considering the husband's personality separately from that of his wife.

In this section we have indicated that we believe a family to have different properties than its members have and that it is important to maintain the distinction between the part and the whole. We have attempted to maintain a balanced presentation by indicating the equal importance to family life of system-level and person-level properties. Effectual family functioning requires that needs at both the system level and the subsystem level be met.

Coalitions

Coalitions are family subsystems that consist of two or more members. Obviously, there must be at least three people in a family for a coalition and, not so obviously, as soon as there are three people, the likelihood exists that a coalition or a series of shifting coalitions will be established.

Coalitions exist, first, because persons have moods and different moods call for different companions; second, because a personality meshes more satisfactorily with one personality than it does with another; and third, because of mutuality of interests. Family members seek to complement their moods, find a satisfying personality complementarity, and advance their interests. Coalitions are established because family members have stronger personality, affectional, functional, or generational ties with some members than they do with others.

In addition, coalitions are inevitable because group well-being and personal well-being cannot always be simultaneously advanced and coalitions are sometimes established around the satisfied-dissatisfied dimension. Family members who are temporarily (or permanently) satisfied will ally themselves, and those who are less satisfied will form a different coalition. Other coalitions grow on different roots. Coalitions can be

based on other dimensions such as "rule makers"/"rule fol-
lowers," "order giver"/"order taker," older generation/
younger generation, spenders/savers, and males/females.

Coalitions are neither unusual nor necessarily divisive. It
is easy to define coalitions as harmful since they seem to split
a family and indicate a lack of unity and harmony. Nevertheless, structural family therapy indicates that unity and harmony can be advanced by the existence of coalitions (Minuchin,
1974). Time and again, Minuchin clearly indicates that effectively functioning families have generationally based coalitions. And, as Nichols (1984) says, "A stable coalition between
the parents will enable them to deal effectively with the
inevitable conflicts with their offspring" (p. 158).

On the other hand, coalitions can destroy effective family
functioning. The idea of "triangulation" points to coalitions
as a source of trouble. Triangulation occurs when two people
are in conflict or have a difference of opinion which they can
neither resolve nor contentedly live with. Each attempts to
make an ally of some other family member in order to "win"
and thereby resolve the matter to his advantage.

Triangulation is most destructive when parents are in
conflict and both try to get the same child on their side.
Triangulation of a child into parental conflict hurts both the
child and the parents. Triangulation hurts the parents because
it serves to stop their conflict without a true resolution. When
a third party is included, the odd-man loses the struggle and
the original difference of opinion is not resolved; it goes
underground and will later surface and again be divisive.

Triangulation diminishes the effectiveness of a family's
functioning by upsetting the control structure. It is in the
nature of systems, person systems included, to attempt to
expand their sphere of influence over others. A child who
is given the opportunity to play off one parent against the
other, and this opportunity will present itself when triangulation occurs, may make the most of it and learn to manipulate
his parents to his advantage. This makes the appropriate
parental guidance and control of the child impossible.

Triangulation hurts children as well. When a child sides
with one parent, he must side against the other and this

seriously disturbs the child's feelings of loyalty and affection. Being intermittently pulled from one parent to the other promotes a situation in which the child sees the world as unstable and unpredictable; being alternately punished and rewarded as the coalitions shift serves to generate a view of the world as the source of pain. The triangulated child has been variously described as a tyrant, a "beanbag" (Albee, 1962), a scapegoat (Vogel & Bell, 1960), or a person with psychosomatic symptoms (Minuchin, 1974).

There are coalitions in the Spencer family and these coalitions are unstable. One coalition includes Mrs. Spencer and Debbie and the two women work together, Mrs. Spencer at home and Debbie at work, to keep Mr. Spencer functioning, or so they think. Mrs. Spencer draws Debbie into a coalition concerning Carolyn's visit and Mr. Spencer is left out of the planning. More often, though, Debbie and Mr. Spencer are in a coalition and Mrs. Spencer is left out. The best example of this is when Mr. Spencer sided with Debbie when Mrs. Spencer was unhappy with her for not getting the party glasses. When Debbie is not present, Mr. Spencer will talk about her disparagingly, as the comments he made to Mrs. Spencer regarding Debbie's incompetence will attest. However, he never enters into a coalition against Debbie when she is present. Apparently, Debbie has achieved virtual spousal status and a strong coalition between Mr. Spencer and Debbie exists.

Considering Carolyn's appearance from the standpoint of coalitions provides some insights into the workings of this family. The first item of interest is that Carolyn attempted to use coalitions so that she could enter the family on a piecemeal basis. Rather than enter into the entire family, she attempted to establish a coalition with Debbie and use that coalition to ease her admission to the family as a whole. She tried different approaches to establish this coalition and she eventually overplayed her hand and Debbie rebuffed her. Then she attempted to establish a coalition with Mr. Spencer and that also was unsuccessful. Carolyn never attempted to get into a coalition with her mother.

Apparently, the structure of the family is so coalition-oriented that the members know that establishing and using coalitions is personally advantageous. Carolyn's lack of success illustrates the problems associated with affecting change in well understood (but shifting) coalition patterns. Her lack of success also indicates that her thinking and behavior are not in line with that of other family members.

The source of some of the Spencer family's problems are indicated by looking at the family from the standpoint of its coalitions. First, there is no strong generational coalition. Debbie is triangulated and sometimes her father and she are in a coalition and, at other times, her mother draws her into one. As we have indicated, coalitions are harmful when they break down intragenerational alignments.

There is no stability in the Spencers' coalitions since they constantly shift. Shifting coalitions can strengthen families when the coalitions are openly entered, when they are not associated with attempts to gain influence, and when they are defined by family members as permissible because they are not associated with ideas of "being left out." But, in the case of the Spencers', the shifting coalitions weaken the family because members get into coalitions for the purpose of gaining influence and because the coalitions involve secrecy, the belittlement of those left out, and disparaging gossip.

Coalitions can enhance family functioning or limit it. Coalitions do the former when executive functions clearly exist as the responsibility and activity of a mutually supportive and well coordinated parental coalition. Coalitions are destructive when the differentiation between generations is blurred, when children are forced to episodically manage their loyalties and affection, and when parental control is weakened because of the desire to win the support of the child.

Information and Family Process

One of the characteristics of a living system is that, at some system level, information is managed. Because a system's adaptation requires a shared and accurate view of the immediate world, its continued existence depends upon the system's ability to handle information. To understand a family's communication processes, it is helpful to understand the terms "information" and "managed."

We will borrow from Bateson to clarify the idea of "information." Bateson (1979) defines information as "any difference that makes a difference" (p. 250) and as "news of difference" (p. 76). Bateson's ideas on information start with the observation that humans and other living things can perceive only that which changes.[25] Lights that flash and police sirens that alter their tone are two examples of the way that perception is enhanced by variation. Or, as Bateson would say, these exemplify the way that perception is made possible by differences: that is, by differences in the signal.

We frequently encounter differences in our environment and we define some as important and some as unimportant. The unimportant differences are sensed, considered, and rejected as inconsequential; unimportant differences may not even be sensed. The information about some change that we consider to be important becomes "news" and is sometimes passed on to others.

The second word requiring further clarification is "managed." The management of information can be accomplished in three major ways. Information can be either (1) generously and accurately expressed or (2) withheld by one member and selectively expressed (or not expressed at all) or (3) distorted (either willfully or not) and distributed in distorted form to others. "Management," then, includes elements of accuracy and expressiveness.

Information management is affected by the characteristics of the involved persons and also by family-level properties. Expressing information, or withholding and distorting it, are at the level of the person. With the generous expression of information, system properties become involved; for the expression of information (a person's activity) becomes communication (a characteristic of the group) when the other family members interact with the sharer and all attempt to agree on the meaning of something. Group properties such as high levels of intimacy and harmony promote a person's sharing. Family properties also affect withholding and distortion in that a family environment characterized by conflict and disorganization will promote secrecy and deception.[26]

Information is usually carried into the family by a member. There are occasions when all family members are simultaneously aware of some difference that affects them all (the destruction of a home by fire), but generally, one family member has the news before some other member. News of a change in the family's context or in the way that family members must carry on transactionally is usually brought to other family members by the member most affected. Similarly, a person's developmental change is brought to other family members when the developing person acts in new ways and thereby gives notice of the inappropriateness of previous ways of interacting.

Family members bring different kinds of information to other family members because each person's life, experiences, and perceptions are unique. Family members have somewhat independent lives outside the family and each person experiences different parts of the world. Even when family members live through a particular situation together, their vantage points and their preconceptions differ and these differences engender different interpretations of the situation. Different family members receive different kinds of information in their transactions with non-family members and they bring this information to other family members.

The way that information is handled in the family requires careful use of the principles established early in this book. The use of the principles to discuss the handling of information may give an overly individualistic view of the family. These two ideas will be considered in the next few paragraphs.

It is tempting to say that a family member brings information to the family. There is an epistemological error in this statement because the family, not possessing a mind, cannot deal with information. To say that a family "handles information" does not help clarify what happens in families because it camouflages such questions as "Who in the family has the information?" "What do these members do with this information?" It is clear that "information is received by the family" creates more problems than it solves.

The same idea could be expressed with an alternative terminology. This terminology would yield the following: "A family member brings information to other family members." There is neither an epistemological error nor an obfuscation because the expression allows "other family members" to be named and indicates that clarity and complete information will be provided only when they are named.

This perspective and terminology creates another problem, however, and that problem, stated as a question, becomes: If we deny that the family is capable of doing such activities as "handling information" and state that only members can do these kinds of things, are we not changing "family" into a "collection of individuals" and thereby eliminating family as an entity. Clearly, if a family is only a collection of individuals and nothing more than that, we are in some difficulty as much of this book would be based on false premises and it would be clear that we need only study psychology to understand family life.

The way out of the difficulty is to acknowledge that family members (1) carry ideas around in their heads, (2) that they express these ideas to other family members, and (3) that the communication which follows allows them to reach an agreement about each one's interpretation of events or whatever the topic happens to be. "Family" is involved in each one of these parts.

The ideas that we carry in our heads are determined by our personality structure (our most basic conscious and unconscious ideas about the world, ourselves, and the other inhabitants) and this structure is, in part, the product of the way that our families of orientation were structured (Henry, 1965).

The expression of one member's ideas to other family members is affected greatly by the way the member with the idea perceives that his ideas will be accepted or otherwise treated. This perception reflects the structure of the family of the present. For example, a person will be unwilling to share information if his perception is that the family structure is so fragile that the information will create disorganization. Harmony, interpersonal conflict, and intimacy are only three of the numerous qualities of families that affect the sharing of information.

The third idea, the negotiation of meaning, also is a family level property. Communication characterized by complementarity is different from that characterized by symmetry, for example, and complementarity and symmetry are family properties. Certainly, the ways that two or more people interact affects both the way they negotiate meaning and their subsequent activities.

We do not rid ourselves of the idea of "family" by being strict in making the distinction between family properties and member properties. On the contrary, we emphasize the importance of "family" as an idea, we illustrate the importance of the family as an entity to be both considered and studied, and we become more able accurately to see the fit between families and members.

Family members deal with incoming information and collectively reach a working agreement either to change their patterns or to maintain them. The process by which the decision is made and the decision itself reflect the family's structure.[27] The working agreement comes from each family member's view of what is wrong, his view of what should be done, his perception of the acceptability of his opinion, and his ability and willingness to act. Ability and willingness to implement the working agreement come from talents, knowledge, and other resources as each member perceives his to be. The powerful family members make a decision, a working agreement, about how they will act and each member's subsequent action is an individualistic rendering of this working agreement.

At the risk of stating the obvious, the Spencer family members are masters at managing information. Mrs. Spencer keeps secrets from Mr. Spencer and protects him that way (Carolyn's residence and visit); Carolyn does not tell anyone in the family that she is coming; Debbie hides from Carolyn the truth about her life; Mr. Spencer protects both Debbie and Mrs. Spencer from the harsh realities of the real world. They are all aware, apparently, that others are keeping secrets but no member does anything to encourage open discussion and full disclosure.

Carolyn might be an exception to the rule that all the Spencers are information managers as, apparently, she tries to give new information by providing another perspective. The perception she brings is not "information" inasmuch as everyone knows the sad state of affairs and her perception is not news. She has no success, since her perspective is rejected because it does not fit the family's mythology. As we have seen, information can come to family members for them to consider and act on only through Mr. Spencer and this he does not allow. Were information shared he would probably reject attempts to act on it.

To summarize, information is carried to the family by individuals and individuals manage the information. Both the working over of the information (that is, the negotiation of the information's importance and meaning) and the decision about subsequent action are collective, not individual, matters. Finally, each member's subsequent activity reflects his personal view of the working agreement.

Thoroughness requires that we include the consideration of Maturana's view of information and contrast his view with that of Bateson. Dell (1985) has performed a valuable service in synthesizing the ideas of these two men and his synthesis is much deeper and richer than that which will be attempted in this abridged and simplified encapsulation. We suggest that students read his excellent article in its entirety.

Bateson's ideas, greatly simplified, are that some event occurs that is perceived and interpreted within the system; the event informs at least part of the system that the system's structure or activities must change if it is to survive. Information comes from outside, part of the system perceives and interprets it, and acts according to both its perception-interpretation and its structure. The system's behavior is the result of its working over of the information. To Bateson, processes of "mind" are extremely important.

Maturana's analysis, on the other hand, holds that a system (every system) is structurally determined (a system's behavior is totally the result of the way "it is made") and that, since its behavior is subject only to internal processes, it receives no input that matters. Within a system's context some perturbation[28] occurs which matches the structure of the system. (The matching will occur if the system's structure is such that the perturbation is allowed to engage some internal part.) The perturbation is not information as such; it is only an event in which there is a joining of part of the system with some part of some other system. Maturana calls this joining "structural coupling."

This part of Maturana's work can be over simplified and summarized as follows. If a system is perturbed in its transactions with other systems, this perturbation is managed within the system and the system's management leads to internal changes that affect its state. Its present state can either be revised or the system can disintegrate (Maturana, 1978). These *internal changes are determined by the structure of the system and not by the perturbation.*

When two systems interact they are "structurally coupled" if they touch each other in any way. If I go to a gas station and get fuel, I become structurally coupled in a brief and superficial way with the attendant; if I am attempting to establish a long-term relationship with a cross-sex individual, the structural coupling is more complicated, encompassing, and multifaceted. In either case, however, structural coupling will occur if we mutually perturb each other.

Consider how Carolyn attempted to structurally couple with Debbie. She tried different approaches (anger, sympathy, affinity, shaming) and none of these worked because they were not acceptable to Debbie's internal structure. Carolyn might have been successful in reaching her sister if she had supported Debbie to the extent of doing Debbie's dirty work, telling Mr. and Mrs. Spencer that Debbie was leaving with her. To do that, however, was impossible for Carolyn because telling her parents was not congruent with either Carolyn's structure or the way that she defined Debbie's problem. (This definition being a result of her structure.) As a result, the sisters could not reach each other and no goal-advancing structural coupling occurred. There was some structural coupling, however, in that Debbie was perturbed to the extent that she ran in tears from the room and Carolyn became upset.

Maturana indicates that systems are structurally plastic and "adaptations arise through the selection of structures that permit the autopoesis (self-production) of the living system in the medium in which it exists" (Maturana, 1978, p. 38).

In other words, a system is not stuck with its internal structure because this structure is constantly being revised as the system experiences its encounters with elements of the real world.

Bateson and Maturana agree that "cause" is not relevant to living systems, that the behavior of living systems is of a piece with other contextual elements, and that behavior is neither cause nor effect. They agree that a system's behavior can be observed as being a response to changes in the environment. This "response" is not viewed in the same way, however. Maturana wrote that a system does not respond, it only *appears* to some observer that the system has responded. Bateson, on the other hand, indicated that adaptation is the system's unique response to contextual change.

The two men agree that it is the structure of the system that determines the effect of the perturbation or trigger and that the trigger's effect is related to the manner in which the system senses and interprets the contextual change. They agree that a system either changes its state and adapts (matches its state with that of the context) or tends toward disintegration. And, finally, both agree that systems tend toward being more richly joined with other parts of their context, to become more complex, and tend to become more highly organized and predictable in their behavior. Their ideas of disagreement (about "mind," "perception," and "information") are significant but should not downplay their agreement on these very important issues.

Closed and Open Systems

In traditional systems analysis, the amount of information entering and leaving a system is usually referred to as the relative "openness" of its boundaries. This relative openness is usually called "boundary permeability" and the more permeable the boundary, the more open the system. As we indicated earlier, neither "boundary" nor "boundary permeability" is a useful term for us but the idea of a system's being more or less open is of utmost importance. "Openness" and "closure" need refinement.

"Openness" and "closure" are at opposite ends of a continuum and no real life families are at the extremes. That is, no family system is either totally open or totally closed. In every family, some information is received and the reception and/or transmission of other information is restricted. Both the amount and the kinds of information that are received and rejected vary from family to family and therefore we use the term "relative openness." "Relative openness" refers to the degree to which a mindful system is receptive to information, and we hope that the reader will remember that "relative openness" always includes "relative closure," that is, some restriction of information.

We believe that the relative openness of a system is defined most usefully as the system's "receptivity to information." A person who is "open" acquires more information than one who is "closed," and in an "open family" the members process (share) more information than in a "relatively closed" family.

A family's relative openness depends on three elements. It depends on its members' acquisition of information, the degree to which this information is accurately and generously shared, and the effectiveness of the process by which the meaning of the information is negotiated.[29]

Some basic ideas about families have here been set forth toward facilitating the understanding of family interaction as it first becomes patterned and then changes over time. But family life remains a mystery until stability and change are understood. With the background to understand these more complex matters now established, we move forward to examine them in depth.

NOTES

17. In everyday language, we frequently use the term "life form" as a synonym for a "species of living things." This term life form is appropriate informal terminology in perfect agreement with our point, that living things have

a form, that the form is characteristic of the species of which the living thing is a member, and the living thing adapts to its context in terms of its genetic endowment and its perception of the best way to advance its own interests.

18. We have not done justice to Bateson's brilliant analysis of the difference between these two kinds of systems. We highly recommend Bateson's *Mind and Nature* (especially his Introduction).

19. The function and purpose of every group affects its interaction patterns and families are no exception. Interaction that occurs in families is different from that in other kinds of groups primarily because the family has different functions than do other groups. Families receive information about what they are supposed to do and this information is different from that which other kinds of social units receive.

20. In the glossary, "cohesion" and "disorganization" are defined and differentiated from, respectively, "integration" and "disintegration."

21. See "Change as a Decrease in Order."

22. Turner's (1970) discussion and classification of family bonds is an important contribution to understanding the integration of family. We recommend his *Family Interaction*, pages 41–96 for a thorough and instructive analysis of the ties that bind family members.

23. In systems analysis, the idea of the differentiation of a system from its context is usually handled with the term "boundary." We prefer not to use the term "boundary" and our rationale is to be found in the glossary.

24. At the risk of being accused of splitting hairs, we would like to clarify the term "family goal" and differentiate it from "family's goal." We will use "family's goal" to refer to a goal on which the members of a particular family agree. For example, when the Spencers were struggling economically, becoming wealthy was their family's goal. The other term, "family goal," will be used

to refer to a goal of the family institution. One such family goal is the meeting of intimacy needs and another is the socialization of the very young.

25. We can sense that which is uniform and that which changes slowly but to sense these nonvariable phenomena we must move our sense receptors. If you will feel some smooth object such as a desk or tabletop, you will find that, after a while, sense reception is enhanced by moving your fingers across the surface.

26. For a more thorough consideration of information management as it occurs in crisis-related behavior, see Montgomery (1981), especially pages 62–68.

27. "Structure" and "working agreement" are perceived as being at different family levels. The working agreement, its process and content, are determined by the structure and being "determined" puts them at a "lower" level.

28. "Perturbation" is a difficult word and some people mistake it for jargon. We will use the word because its meaning of "throw into disorder" is exactly what we wish to express. Synonyms for perturbation are "jolt," "shock," and "disturb," but these words do not quite express what we wish to express, the idea that a system can be affected by some outside force if the system's structure is such that the force can be felt.

29. Frequently, systems analysis includes in "openness" the way that the family acts on the information; but we do not include adaptation as a part of "relative openness." See "Boundary" in the glossary for a treatment of this issue.

Chapter 4

STABILITY AND CHANGE

Two people meet and each one consciously or unconsciously decides that a relationship with the other will enable him or her to get their intimacy needs met. As they begin to build their relationship, society provides them with a set of guidelines that defines "family" for them and thereby prescribes the organization of their relationship. Within these guidelines they create a structure that fits their particular personalities and their unique circumstances.

Having established a family system, the two people must work to solve two new problems which emerge. The first problem has to do with maintaining the system's integration. As we have seen, integration is a problem because a person, being able to survive as a single entity, can leave a particular relationship and attempt to get his needs met somewhere else. The second issue has to do with adaptation and arises from the fact that changes in the family's context, changes in members, and changes in relationships necessarily will occur and these changes will have to be handled in some way.

This leads us to inquire into what are, in all likelihood, the two most important and least understood features of living systems: stability and change. In physical systems, stability and change are handled easily and well, for all practical purposes, by Newton's familiar laws—those having to do with a body at rest remaining at rest and a body in motion continuing to move until acted upon by some force.

Living systems are not as tidy as physical systems, since living systems have internal resources and processes and these complicate system stability and change. A stone has no biography, no experience, no mind, and neither thought nor genetically programmed responses. A living system has some or all of these characteristics and, because it has, its method of dealing with outside forces that threaten either its stability or development is quite different from that of stonelike things.

To understand the world of living systems, especially family systems, we must inquire into the nature of the reciprocal characteristics of stability and change. This inquiry will proceed by considering the way that ideas about stability and change are related to ideas about structure and organization and to ideas about the source of the "trigger," the change impetus. We will then consider what it *is* that changes and how change and stability occur. In the last part of the book we will consider stages of system development.

STRUCTURE AND ORGANIZATION

A System Develops from Chaos to Order

Consider a group of students, an entire class entering university. It is fall and we can imagine them all attending an orientation for first-year students. If we catch them early, we may be able to see them before pairs of persons begin to appear. At the very first, the group of students appears to be a collection of individuals, some kind of mass, and the only differentiation between individuals in this mass is associated with personal attributes and sex-related characteristics.

As we watch this group over the 4 years of the university career, we can see pairs of persons become differentiated from the mass. Those that fit our frame of reference are pair members of different gender who have joined with their pair-mates to get their intimacy needs met and/or to establish long-term family relationships.

In order to get these needs met, the members of each couple go through a series of steps. Roughly stated, the steps are as follows. First, they find a cross-sex person who appears to be compatible; they begin to spend time together; concurrently with that, they begin to negotiate the way each wants the relationship to be structured and they attempt to arrive at some mutually agreeable arrangement; they begin to restrict their leisure time activities to the other person; they begin to see themselves as part of a couple. As these developments occur, progress is marked by greater self-disclosure, greater evidence of commitment, and increasingly frequent and intense sexual interaction. These increases in disclosure, commitment, and in sexual interaction indicate progress to the pair; to outsiders progress is indicated by movement through a series of publicly accepted stages. These include "going steady," being engaged, etc.

From the systems standpoint, what is happening here is that the pair is differentiating itself from the mass of students and the persons within the pair are becoming *less* differentiated from each other. In other words, the couple becomes more and more separate from others and less and less separate from each other.

Systems begin with internal chaos and transactional non-differentiation and move toward interactional order and contextual differentiation. In family terms, two strangers meet and begin to interact. Most of each person's behavior is a mystery to the other and their interaction is generally tentative, disordered, and random. Gender and age roles and cues from each person's self-presentation provide a basis for whatever initial order exists.

Language commonalities allow for the negotiation of attendant confusions and for working out the inevitable differences in expectations. Negotiation will occur to the extent that the participants believe that negotiation will advance a relationship in which their personal goals and needs can be met. With successful negotiation, more areas of interaction open up, more intense feelings characterize their mutual involvement, and expectations regarding interaction become established. The result is patterned behavior; that is, repeated interaction sequences.

As a family system develops, interaction sequences that "work" (that is, that meet the needs of family members) are repeated. The better that the interaction sequence works, the more likely it is to be repeated. That which works in a satisfactory manner is more often repeated than that which does not work as well. More complex, frequent, and intense interaction evolves and the developing system becomes more complicated. Establishing some interactional order is necessary or the system will die of its internal confusions and the concomitant behavioral dissonance. Developing systems move from chaos toward order, from random to patterned behavioral sequences.

As the couple develops an internal order it also becomes an identifiable unit, one that is differentiated from the mass of unattached persons and separate from other family units. In the beginning, the persons are not part of a couple; they are individuals and they do not exist as a unit. With continuing interaction, their connections with each other become more ordered (predictable) and they begin to see themselves as a couple. Also, other people recognize them as a separate entity. Becoming a family has these two aspects: first, increasing interactional order and unity and, second, increasing transactional differentiation.

"Organization" Defined

Each person in this developing relationship expects that, if all goes well, a family will result. Each expects that he will be treated in a particular familial way, that he will be able to accomplish certain goals, and that he will be able to give and receive elements of self in a fashion specific to families. The two people are not forming a street gang or a political party or a basketball team or a family studies department. They are forming a family and the characteristics of a family, as these characteristics are defined by society, specify the organization of their dyad. The organization of their particular group will be typical of families in general.

"Organization," then, is that particular arrangement of persons and their interaction that makes it possible for them to do what they are "supposed" to do. A family group's organization identifies it as a family. In other words, the identification of a system as being of a particular type is based on the system's organization. If a group's organization is such that, within it, its members' intimacy needs are met, reproductive-type activity occurs, and other family-specific personal and societal functions are met, that group is organized along family lines and is called a family.

According to Maturana (1978), a system has an organization dictated by the socially prescribed functions that the system fulfills for its members and for society. The system's organization is a whole, an irreducible entity which is fixed. This does not allow for much freedom on the part of its members, but, lest we become pessimistic, let us consider elements of structure.

"Structure" Defined

In a developing relationship, the persons organize themselves according to general cultural principles and basic human needs. As they strive to meet these organizational requirements their relationship takes on a unique shape. This unique shape is the relationship's "structure." Each person's behavior meshes with the other's behavior in a way that is specific to the pair. They play the paired roles (lover-lover, engaged couple, husband-wife) of intimate relationships in a unique way; they decide issues and solve problems in a way which they share with no other pair. No two biological systems, even those with the same organization, have the same structure; no two families are the same in their structure, because the members are unique in their personalities and the particular *mix* of personalities that results from their handling of personal idiosyncrasies can never be duplicated.

As examples of structure, consider symmetry and complementariness (Watzlawick et al., 1967). A family can fulfill its organizationally prescribed functions in a variety of ways; different families use different structures. One type of family structure is characterized by complementary interaction. In complementary interaction, the behavior of the people fits in that each person does the opposite or reciprocal of what the other does. One gives and the other takes, one is pessimistic and the other is optimistic. If one is dependent, the other must be domineering; if one is assertive, the other will be retiring. Many relationships are characterized by complementariness: student-teacher, traditional doctor/patient, and traditional husband/wife. A marital relationship characterized by complementariness (such as that of Mr. and Mrs. Spencer) can work very well and fulfill its organizational requirements. It can also be personally satisfying if the personalities of the family members are such that each member wants this particular type of interaction structure.

Complementary interaction is very different from symmetrical interaction. In complementary parts of relationships, there are two positions. One is the "one-up" position and the other is called the "one-down" position.[30] In symmetrical relationships, no such reciprocal positions exist. In symmetrical relationships, neither party is willing to be less than the other in any regard, not less powerful, not less angry, not less caring or witty or knowledgeable. Symmetrical relationships are based on similarity rather than difference. In symmetrical relationships, there is more sharing, more mutuality, and more competition than there is in relationships marked by complementariness.

Relationships characterized by symmetry can be as successful as those characterized by complementariness. Families with a predominance of either type of pattern are able to meet socially prescribed organizational requirements and can satisfy family members. Family success requires only that the family members' personalities be such that they can work together in reasonable harmony and that each can thrive because basic needs are being met within the particular family structure that has evolved.

Symmetry and complementariness are structural elements in that families develop a particular interactional style within their organizational requirements. The style that evolves depends upon the characteristics of the persons. It is *"their business"* how they structure their interaction, and outsiders have little to say as long as organizational requirements are met.

Structure allows us to see the system's parts and the relationships among these parts (Maturana, 1978). The structure of a family has to do with such familiar ideas as the way that members' behaviors fit together and the particular way that the members interact. Consideration of family structure includes such elements as roles, division of labor, and the management of information.

The term "organization" refers rather to the general and holistic manner in which the family is established and the principles and task requirements on which it is based. A family's *organization cannot be taken apart and analyzed;* a group is either a family or it is not. "Structure," on the other hand, allows us to analyze what happens within the system and it is through *structure* that we see how each family accomplishes the tasks that are required by its socially prescribed *organization.*

The Spencer family is organizationally a family in that it accomplishes what families are supposed to accomplish and it is recognized as a family by members and outsiders. Intimacy needs are met, members' needs are provided for, the protection of members occurs, some socialization occurs, and we can guess that some sexual interaction occurs between Mr. and Mrs. Spencer. Despite both the existence of dysfunction and the change in functions that has occurred, the Spencers are intimate and this intimacy points to the continued existence of family type organization. The evidence of *dysfunction* does not mean that the group is *not organized as a family.*

As you can tell by comparing your family with the Spencers, the Spencers are unique. The special circumstances in the members' biographies, the singular mix of personalities, their once-only position in time and space, and the way these factors have been combined give the Spencers a structure that can never be duplicated. In their attempts to be a family, they have created a set of patterns that allow them to continue as a unit, to do what they must do to satisfy society's family requirements, and to meet the members' needs. The Spencers have established a singular structure.

Some of the Spencer family's interaction is primarily characterized by complementariness. In the short-lived argument regarding Mrs. Spencer's writing the check for which there were insufficient funds, Mrs. Spencer immediately, virtually automatically, took the one-down position and Mr. Spencer was one-up. Interaction between Mr. Spencer and Debbie is primarily complementary as well.

When Carolyn is involved in dyadic interaction the situation is quite different as symmetry replaces complementarity as the dominant mode. Carolyn's interaction with her father is primarily symmetrical and much of their interaction in the last part of the play is concerned with the characteristic escalation of this symmetrical pattern; the runaway escalation is stopped when both Carolyn and her father agree about the nature of the interaction within the family and that there is nothing to be done to improve the interaction. (Carolyn's "I guess that's it, then" and her father's subsequent statement marks the end of the escalation.)

Carolyn's interaction with her sister is poorly defined as to complementariness and symmetry and this poor definition is one reason their conversation turns out badly. When Carolyn started her discusssion with Debbie she indicated that she wanted a symmetrical relationship. This was indicated in several ways: Carolyn's desire to "Let's talk for a minute," and her "Sit for a minute with me" and the sharing of the party food. The confusion was introduced by Carolyn's complementary expressions and Debbie's acquiescence. For example, when Debbie was going to announce Carolyn's arrival, Carolyn ordered Debbie not to. When Debbie obeyed, complementariness (Carolyn's order combined with Debbie's compliance) was established. Complementariness was also introduced by Carolyn's questioning Debbie and Debbie's responding. The nature of Debbie and Carolyn's interaction became confused as the wish for symmetry was expressed complementarily. Since a relationship cannot be simultaneously both complementary and symmetrical and since the lack of a clear definition of mode is a barrier to interactional success, the unsatisfactory outcome of the interaction was set at the beginning.

WHAT TRIGGERS CHANGE

It should be amply clear by now that the impetus to change is a trigger and not a cause (Bateson, 1979). A child develops and other family members must somehow adapt to the child's new behavior and members' adaptation will be associated with new patterns of interaction. The child says, in effect, "Here is a new part of me, what are you going to do about it?" Or, society changes and says, "Your job is gone, how are you going to handle family finances?" Some situation or event or occasion asks the family members a question about whether they are able or ready or willing to change and whether they can adjust as a group to the new reality. The family and its members behaviorally answer the question by processing or not processing information and by acting or not acting on that information.

The event that triggers family change comes from either *outside* the family or from *inside* the family, but from a *different system level*. An example of a transactional trigger would be something as obvious as the destruction of the family home by a tornado or the breadwinner's loss of job. Virtually all families, especially those in a rapidly changing society such as ours, are subject to natural and social vicissitudes over which the family has no control.

Triggers also come from within the family, from changes in persons, and from changes in family relationships. Examples of these changes from within are the maturation of a child, the death of a family member, or the decision and subsequent action of parents to support each other more strongly. Each of these events would tend to change the family's interaction; each comes from within the family but not at the family system level.

Regardless of source, events that trigger change are vital parts of family's life. Triggers keep family members alert and responsive to contextual elements; triggers prevent family patterns from becoming routine, predictable, and dull. Triggers tend to perturb the family system by indicating some difference in the family's circumstances with which members or the family as a whole must deal. Obviously, the way that persons and families deal with triggers has to do with stability and change.

BALANCING CHANGE AND STABILITY

We have seen that family interaction becomes structured as the system is organized to meet society's requirements and members' needs. Ideas of fairness might suggest that after a couple has put a structure in place, its situation would settle down and the members could live happily ever after. Experience indicates, however, that being left alone is a gift infrequently bestowed on families. Change in the context, change in one of the member's characterstics, and changes in internal relationships are facts of life and no family can avoid them.

Change is necessary, but so is stability. Theorists have indicated that the survival of a living system requires both processes (Maruyama, 1968; Speer, 1970). A family cannot adapt indiscriminately without destroying its essence and its reason for being. It means something to be a Fewer or a Montgomery or a Spencer; this meaning takes years to be established and it is an important component of the identity of each family member. Adaptation that changes the family's meaning destroys the family and dramatically affects the self-image of each member. Dramatic changes of this nature are generally resisted by family members.

A family's changing its patterns can be either functional or dysfunctional for that family. Pattern change supports the continuation and strength of a family when its inappropriate patterns (those that no longer do what they were intended to do) are revised. Change is dysfunctional when structural revision occurs which is either unnecessary or misdirected (Watzlawick, Weakland, & Fisch, 1974). An example of unnecessary pattern revision is an attempt to completely eliminate conflict; misdirected revision is exemplified by the scapegoating of a child to deflect spousal hostility.

As noted, a family's maintaining stability can be either functional or dysfunctional. Stability is functional when the system's patterns are doing what they were intended to do and when the continuity of values and behavior within the system promotes predictability and a sense of identity among the members. Stability is dysfunctional when ineffective transactional and interactional patterns are maintained and these ineffective patterns weaken either the family members' or the family's ability to function (Montgomery, 1981).

From the standpoint of the balance between stability and change existing in the family, it should be clear that the Spencer family does not work very well. Indicators of dysfunction are Debbie's inability to gain her independence, Mrs. Spencer's use of symptomatic behavior (which in itself is debilitating) to control others' behavior, the management of information within the family, Mr. Spencer's single-minded pursuit of financial gain, and a low level of intimacy.

All families show evidence of both good and ill health and, like other families, the Spencers show signs of being able to function ably as well as of being dysfunctional. The members are safe in the home, the members (at least Mr. Spencer) carry on ably outside the home, no one in the family engages in crime, and the family itself is an important part of the community. One daughter has managed to move away from home and to function fully as an adult in a distant community. In many ways, the Spencers do what families are supposed to do.

Each of the Spencers, except Carolyn, has a personal stake in maintaining the family as it is and this desire for stability makes any change of the family's ways unlikely. The Spencers have not changed very much over the years as, apparently, a deal was made some time previously which helped both Mr. and Mrs. Spencer to get their personal needs met. These needs have been met and, since the needs have not changed, the family system has continued and its patterns have emphasized stability rather than adaptability.

Obviously, Carolyn is a "trigger" and the potential change agent. Her focus is not on the advantages of stability but on its costs, especially as these costs are paid by Debbie. Carolyn is emphatic toward Debbie who, as Carolyn projects, is experiencing the same kinds of personal sacrifice and malaise that Carolyn felt over the years. Carolyn wants to change the family or at least "rescue" Debbie but her failure is guaranteed because neither Debbie nor her father or mother want the situation to change. Carolyn is unable to indicate to the other family members the way that change would be advantageous for them and, as a result, her attempts to trigger change are ineffective.

The Spencers value family stability and the resulting integration and continuity more than they value each person's well-being and ability to grow as individuals. It is unlikely that the Spencers will change unless personal dysfunction disturbs the family's patterns in some momentous way or some other trigger upsets family interaction or transaction patterns.

WHAT CHANGES, WHAT IS UNCHANGING

In themselves, the terms "stability" and "change" are essentially meaningless; they only have meaning when applied to specific family processes. In the next section we will consider how stability and change are related to the organization and structure of systems.

Structural Change

Structural change occurs if a family accommodates to some contextual or member's change without its organization being affected. With structural change, the way that components fit together is revised; the family continues to be recognized as a family. The Spencers changed structurally when Carolyn left. Mrs. Spencer got sick and became as a child, Debbie took over the house and acted in the parent role. The family continued to act as a family. This role reversal with continued organizational integrity is an example of change.

Since members fit together in a great many different ways, "structural change" requires further delimitation. The way that the behavior of members fits together and becomes patterned is the essence of structure and this matched behavior has to do with the way that tasks are accomplished (the division of labor), the predominant style of interaction (complementary or symmetrical, separate or enmeshed), transactional openness, and information management. Structural change means that the relationship among the components in one of these areas has been changed and that the change will be reflected in other parts of the structure. The family that structurally changes continues with its same *organization*, but it *operates* in a different fashion.

Organizational Change

With organizational change, a system either ceases to exist or it becomes a new system; its parts are divested of their unifying connections and the parts are assembled anew into different organizational forms (Maturana, 1978; Dell, 1982). Organizational change means that a family no longer exists as a family. Since organization is what sets a family apart from other groups, a collection of persons that no longer accomplishes what we expect to have accomplished in families is no longer a family. With organizational change, there is system discontinuity.

In broad strokes, the difference between structural and organizational change seems clear, but when specific matters are considered the picture becomes blurred. If a family dyad disintegrates and the spouses go their separate ways, the change is an organizational one. On the other hand, if the relationship between a father and a son reflects the increased independence of the son and mutuality replaces dominance and submission as the characteristic mode of father and son interaction, then a structural change has occurred. The relationship between the father and son remains intimate. Intimacy persists because of, not despite, the interaction patterns being changed.

Other situations are not as easily classified. For example, can a change in family personnel be classified as merely a structural change if the family remains organizationally sound? Does a single-parent family differ structurally or organizationally from a two-parent family? Does the birth of a child change the family's organization or just its structure? Obviously, we do not have the verbal tools to draw fine lines so we must make an arbitrary decision. To wit, an intact family which changes and remains identifiable as a family has experienced structural changes only. A group which has changed so much that it no longer exists as a family has undergone an organizational change.

STABILITY AND THE POWER OF PRECEDENTS

Both structural stability and organizational stability are related to the influence of precedents. That is, if precedents influence behavior more than do current circumstances, the family will tend to be stable. In fact, "structural stability" and the "power of precedents" are two ways of saying the same thing: Some systems change their structure very slowly and structural change occurs only under extreme conditions. The system's initial structure predominates over current requirements.

Families on the closed end of the open/closed continuum have members and interaction processes that limit the amount of accurate information made available to family members. With restrictive information management, news that some change has subverted once-effective patterns fails to trigger adaptation and the patterns that have become inappropriate are not corrected.

The more a system is closed, the more that its behavior and the behavior of its subsystems are affected by its initial structure. How could it be otherwise? With a minimum of information coming in and being processed, precedents will be followed, since they comprise the only reference for judging the value of interaction patterns and the family's way of life.

Families that are structurally stable are guided by the past, by precedents that began with the system's initial structure.

Ordinality

To put this issue into formal terminology, stability has to do with issues of "ordinality." Ordinality is a term we have coined to indicate the tendency specified by Kaplan that, ". . . we must do as we aspire from the very beginning, or else resign ourselves to not doing [it] at all" (1964, p. 402). In other words, it is the initial steps, the first structure, the precedents, that determine subsequent structure.

According to the "principle of ordinality," there is a tendency in systems for patterns, processes, and behavior to be repeated and the system's end is mechanistically determined (or, less extremely stated, "affected") by its initial processes. As Bateson says, ". . . the shape of what happened between you and me yesterday carries over to shape how we respond to each other today" (1979, p. 16). Any structural change that occurs will be constrained by prior ways of interacting and will depart only slightly from the prior ways. The tendency toward ordinality makes any change a continuation of preceding structure; discontinuous change is impossible unless there is a new organizational configuration.

Coherence

Dell's idea of "coherence" fits well with the idea of ordinality. By coherence Dell means that each system has its own particular structure and acts only in ways specified by its singular identity and the unique fit of its components. Present behavior is congruent with past behavior and behavior reflects the same (although evolving) structure and identity. "Coherence" is associated with the continued life of a system and pattern "discontinuity" means that the system has died; that is, that the system has been transformed and a new system (or systems) has been created.

The idea of coherence helps to clarify the matter of family system stability. Issues of stability and change begin when a family member senses some difference in self or context and acts on the news. His actions, although changed, will be congruent with his personality. His new behaviors will trigger changes in the other family members with whom he now relates differently and his new mode will not fit with the other family members' views of the way things ought to be. The behavior of the changed family member is not totally understandable to the others, for the others do not have the same information. Moreover, their coherence is affected and they (usually) attempt to reestablish former interaction patterns.

If the others are to continue their interaction with the changed person, they must either eliminate the new behavior or adapt to it. Adaptation upsets their own coherence; therefore their first response is usually one of resistance. Family members resist another member for the reason that change requires them to rethink their ideas about the changed person, about interaction, and about themselves. Predictability is upset, and what was previously done easily and automatically must now be done consciously and with effort.

There is another reason that persons minimize the change in others. Although much of life has to do with family participation, there is still a substantial part of each person's life that is nonfamilial. Persons must harmonize the family and nonfamily aspects of their lives and sometimes a change in the family part is resisted because it will require an unacceptable change in the work part and vice versa. Consequently, changes in the family are acted upon in such a way that their effect on nonfamily behavior will be minimized. For example, a husband may resist increased family involvement if this extra commitment means less opportunity to succeed in business or to socialize with friends.

Considering the Spencers from the standpoint of ordinality, coherence, and the power of precedents yields the following analysis. Within the Spencer family there are well developed patterns that limit the flow of information and thereby "close" the family. Being essentially a closed system, the Spencer family and each of the people in it are subject to the tendency of ordinality.

There seems to be one part of the Spencer family's history that does not fit the pattern of closedness and ordinality. That part is the skeleton in the closet, the relationship between Mr. Spencer and Mrs. Simpson. It appears that the Simpsons and the Spencers had been close and that there was much openness between the four people but that this changed when the "deal" was struck between Mr. and Mrs. Spencer. The principle of ordinality as well as ideas of coherence would suggest that this early openness would continue and, since openness engenders more openness, the open nature of the family would increase.

It could be that *Silver Anniversary*, being incongruent with "the way things are," is written incorrectly. But on the evidence of the present version, let us contemplate another explanation. Both Mr. and Mrs. Spencer view this part of their lives with the Simpsons as a "special" time and that *specialness* would suggest that the time was not consistent with the part of their life that preceded it and that followed. It might be that this "daredevil stage" was not congruent with the values and behavior of both Mr. and Mrs. Spencer and that the closedness and inflexibility (the most essential characteristics of each Spencer) eventually came to the fore and the Simpsons were eliminated from active involvement in the Spencers' lives.

It would appear that the trial-and-error processes that are a part of life frequently generate similar circumstances. Frequently, a person, or some other system, will attempt something "new." This new attempt to adapt will follow from the system's structure (it will be coherent) and if it "works," the system's structure will change, but only a little, to accommodate the new kind of adaptation. If the adaptation attempt does not work, or if it is too far removed from basic values, the new behavior will not become a part of the system because the existing structure will reject it.

We see coherence time and time again in the script. It is indicated that Carolyn's previous exit from the family came about for the reason that her structure gave rise to behavior and a concomitant view of reality that was not shared and which she, like the other family members, was unwilling to change. When she left, her absence changed the personnel and interactional aspects of the family's structure. However, the agreed-upon perception of reality was not affected and new interaction sequences were created to maintain this perception and the related behavior. The new interaction sequences included Mrs. Spencer's illness and Debbie's increased involvement in managing the family.

System Equilibration and Levels

System stability, frequently referred to as "homeostasis," is the maintenance of a steady state, an equilibrium. Dell's (1982) attack on homeostasis, in which he indicates the term's uselessness and epistemological impurity, makes sense to us and we see no reason to continue using the term. Despite our agreement with Dell about homeostasis, our analysis of stability differs from his.

Dell interprets Hoffman as making "homeostasis a characteristic of the system as a whole" (1982, p. 24) and he suggests that this is an improvement over previous dualistic thinking. Dell, thereby posits equilibration at the system level. This position, that equilibration is at the system level, is problematic, since Dell later says that a system qua system changes. Actually, he does not say this in so many words. What he says is, ". . . in living systems, order spontaneously arises" (1982, p. 36). The increase in order is a systemic change for order is a system-level property. The problem, then, is that change and stability are both seen as being "natural" tendencies that occur at the systems level. To say that a system is both naturally equilibrating and naturally developing is akin to saying that some object is both all blue and all red.

Our analysis avoids this particular problem by making stability a subsystem function and by making the development of complexity a property of the system. As Land put it, ". . . [homeostasis] is true for parts of the systems, it is never true of a whole system" (Land & Kenneally, 1977, p. 17). Also, Haley's "first law" states that "When one person indicates a change in relation to another, the other will act upon the first so as to diminish and modify that change" (Haley, 1963,

p. 189). Family stability is accomplished by members; family development (increased complexity) occurs at the system level.

Thus family stability is the result of the interplay among the personal systems of which it is comprised. And, when family members minimize the effect of change in other family members, they bring stability to the system and greater complexity as well.

Seeing stability as being a subsystem property makes it possible to avoid dualistic thinking. Instead of saying that one member stabilizes the family (a dualism), we say that a family's stability comes about because of family members' interaction. We say that the system remains stable (that is, adapts slowly) because, to paraphrase Hoffman, some interaction sequence *among members* serves a change-resistant function (Hoffman, 1976, p. 502).

The Spencer family is remarkably stable and the interaction among the members is such that stability is maintained. We have pointed out how the shifting coalitions help preserve the family's stability and how information is managed so that the family stays on an even keel. In addition, there are numerous examples of how the potential effect of the deviation in perspective brought by Carolyn is minimized in different ways by Debbie (panic), Mrs. Spencer (withdrawal into symptomatic behavior), and Mr. Spencer (belligerence). It should be emphasized that the techniques used to engender stability are at the sub-family system level.

CHANGE

We know that individuals and families change and this fact reminds us that stability is not the whole picture. Structural change is a part of the daily life of all systems; organizational change, although less common, occurs with sufficient frequency to be familiar to all of us. In this section, we will look at change in terms of a system's increasing both its complexity and its order. We will also consider change as an increase in disorder. We will focus on the sources of change and the system's degree of openness. Also, we will look at the related ideas of orders of change, positive feedback loops, and system discontinuity.

Change as an Increase in Complexity and Order

As we have seen, systems change in that they become more ordered, more complex. One reason for the increase in the complexity of systems such as the family (systems which are composed of parts that can exist independently) is that the parts have separate lives, unique experiences, and idiosyncratic growth patterns. Each of the parts is capable of independent change.

When the changed person interacts in a new way with some other family member, the system's complexity is increased. Family members can act to minimize the effect of the new behavior or they can accept the new behavior and adapt to it. In either case, the system's complexity will increase; neither the changed person nor other family members can return to their former state.

If the changed behavior is accepted by another family member, and accommodation to the new behavior takes place, new interaction sequences (the new behavior, the accommodation, the mix of the two) are created. After the two people who are immediately involved have worked out mutually acceptable patterns, other members will become involved as the ever widening circle of involvement touches their lives.

If the second person acts to minimize the first person's change, complexity is increased because the minimizing behavior is an addition to the total of family interaction. The minimizing behavior is new; something has been added. Moreover, the minimizing behavior is ordinarily met by a counterresponse on the part of the changing person and this countermove is also new. On and on it goes, as new and more complex interaction sequences develop and as other family members are affected, since the moves and countermoves affect interaction sequences among other family members.

To summarize, the change of an individual brings about greater complexity in the system because, whether it is ac-

cepted or not, new behavior generates secondary accommo-
dating behavior which is unprecedented and which requires
that persons add new perceptions to their worldview and new
behaviors to their repertoire. With new thinking and new
behavior, more complex interaction sequences will emerge,
the new interaction sequences being in tune with the new
reality.

The Spencers, who maintain stability at virtually all cost,
provide numerous examples of these ideas. We are told by
Debbie about the increased complexity of family interaction,
and when Mrs. Spencer became ill when Carolyn left, roles
were redistributed, new interaction sequences went into effect,
and the family members' interactions were altered and rees-
tablished in more complex ways. Family members' nonac-
ceptance of change also leads to complexity. When Carolyn
entered the picture, the other three members acted to minimize the effect of her deviant perspective. Debbie got agitated, Mrs. Spencer took refuge in one of her "attacks," and
Mr. Spencer became bullying. Eventually, all three members
formed a coalition that excluded her and Carolyn was left
alone in the kitchen. The panic, withdrawal, and belligerence,
although part of each person's standard strategy for dealing
with the world, complicated family interaction in that they
were utilized to adapt to a new situation (Carolyn's return)
and, being added to the family's repertoire, the complexity
of the family members' interaction increased. Paradoxically,
family stability is accomplished by greater complexity of the
system. Inasmuch as an increase in complexity is a system
change, it can be said that family (organizational) stability is
accomplished by family (structural) change.

Another reason for a system's increase in complexity is
simply that it is in the nature of living things to attempt to
make for themselves as *large* a place as they can and to *extend*
themselves over time. The preceding statement comes per-
ilously close to breaking our rule regarding the avoidance of
nonexplanations. But observation and experience do seem to
indicate the truth of this statement and we may have to be
satisfied with experiential data. We mean that we do not, for
example, know why a tree grows, but we know that it does;

this knowledge may not be satisfying but it is all that we have. In the same vein, we do not know why a person or a family grows.

The final explanation for the increase in order in family systems is that the members desire to reduce the amount of conscious thought required for dealing with day-to-day living. There seems to be a tendency for humans to attempt to maximize automatic behavior (Koestler, 1978). Habitual behavior and known expectations lead to predictable interaction and this predictability allows persons to deal with the trivia of daily life without consciously thinking about them. This is beneficial because rational and conscious decision-making abilities are thereby made available for creative and other complex mental functions; persons can transcend mere coping and act to substantially improve their lives.

Change as a Decrease in Order

System disorganization can be attributed to four factors: entropic deterioration, the failure of structure to accommodate the changes in complexity, the furthering of a component's well-being to the system's detriment, and the system's destruction of the ecology that nurtures it.

The second law of thermodynamics, ". . . the Entropy Law, states that matter and energy can only be changed in one direction . . . from ordered to disordered" (Rifkin, 1980, p. 6). Mountains are reduced to rubble, energy which was once available becomes unavailable, and after death the human body becomes undifferentiated from the earth into which it was placed.

While it is true that entropy refers to physical systems and, as Dell (1982) says, it does not apply to living systems, it does apply to parts of living systems. As we have seen, living systems "break" the entropy law in that they become more ordered. At the same time the physical parts of living systems, being subject to physical laws, wear out and no longer work. The continued existence of the whole system requires that these parts be replaced; repair and replacement are common. Eventually, the corrective measures lose their ability to regenerate and the system tends toward disorganization. We call this "aging."

Secondly, systems deteriorate because they fail to adapt their structure to meet the new demands created by their increased size and complexity. Call it administration, or management, or coordination, but, by whatever name, the activities of system components must be integrated or the resulting inability to get things done will destroy the system. Doing one's own thing is an attractive idea but if each person does his own thing and these "own things" are not coordinated or related to some central theme, the system will be brought down.

The integration of the activities of a system's parts can be accomplished in a number of ways. A central figure can direct the activities or a hierarchy can develop that will coordinate behavior. In small systems, an agreement can be made among the system's components and members' actions can reflect that agreement. Integration of activities is essential to a system's well-being and the method of integration depends on the system's size, its organization, and its structure.[31]

We are not saying that all behavior in a system must be perfectly and harmoniously integrated. A system's well-being also requires unpredictability, random behavior, and experimentation. The unusual behavior and thinking will produce disharmony, but it also generates new interactional and transactional sequences that may become parts of the family's behavioral repertoire. The more behavioral and mental alternatives that family members know, the more intelligent the decision that can be made.

To summarize, a system's internal structure must develop as fast as does its increasing complexity. If structure lags behind the increase in complexity, a system will deteriorate because its members and coalitions will not work together in a harmonious fashion and because its transactions will also be ineffective. That is, outsiders may disrupt the system or information may not be received.

The third source of system deterioration is to be found in the parts becoming so imperialistic, selfish, and self-serving that they weaken the whole for their own aggrandizement.

As we have seen, the properties of the parts are not those of the whole and a system's parts can take too much for themselves and not leave enough for the other parts or for the whole system. Dictators who have used the wealth of their domains to further their private interests, family tyrants (a spouse or a parent or a child) who demand that everything be done their way, and a section of society (agriculture or business or labor) which takes from other segments to ensure its own well-being are all examples of the part taking precedence over the whole. A system, if it is to exist and work effectively, must have some agency that will control those parts which wish to exploit the system for their own benefit.

The fourth source of deterioration in living systems is to be found in the system's transactions. A system is doomed if it fails to protect the environment in which it grows and on which it depends. We have attempted to show that systems become larger and more complex and that they do so by using resources that the context provides for them. However, it is essential that a system protect and maintain its context, for its existence depends on it. A family system that uses a particular field for food cannot destroy the food-bearing quality of the field without placing its own continuity in jeopardy. This is, of course, also true for larger social systems.

In the preceding sections, we have indicated that systems grow in that they become more ordered and that systems also tend to deteriorate and they become disordered. We now move on to consider change in terms of openness and, finally, to indicate kinds of change and system discontinuity.

Open Systems and Change

We recall that the relative openness of a system has to do with (1) the ability of its members to sense changes accurately, (2) the accuracy and generality of the information dissemination within the family, and (3) the success of the members in reaching consensus about the meaning of the information. An open system is not as affected by its initial organization and by precedents as is a closed system for the reason that the handling of information within an open system allows the system to separate itself from its beginnings. Openness makes adaptation possible. A system separates itself from its initial organization by acting on the contextual and internal information which has been taken in and processed.

Open people and open families tend to be creative in the use of information and in the establishment of new patterns that are congruent with new circumstances. Open systems can create new alternatives and establish new patterns that fit, not so much with the old structure, but with the new context. In open systems, precedents do not determine behavior and coherence is more difficult to see.

The open system counterpart of "ordinality" is "equifinality." As Watzlawick et al. (1967) explain it, ". . . equifinality means that the same results may spring from different origins, because it is the nature of the organization which is predeterminate. . . . This corollary rests on the premise that [current] system parameters will predominate over initial conditions" (p. 127). Equifinality is the idea that *ends and beginnings can be independent.* That is, systems with a common beginning can have end states that are very different; systems with a similar end state can develop from widely divergent sources. This view of systems provides for the existence of unprecedented behavior; it allows for the possibility that open and thoughtfully creative systems can act in new ways.

Systems display both of the tendencies, ordinality and equifinality, and the relative power of the tendencies is related to the degree of openness and closedness of the system. The more open the system, the stronger will be the tendency toward equifinality. The more that the system is closed, the more powerful will be the tendency toward ordinality.

Similarly, the tendency toward ordinality can be expected to be stronger in systems that are large in size (a three-generation family with a full contingent of aunts, uncles, cousins, grandparents, etc.) rather than those that are small (a two-person nuclear family); systems that are complex in structure (families with a structured division of labor with much specialization) rather than more simple structured systems (families with a loose labor structure with members who are generally able to perform tasks); and systems in which the members are interactionally active and close (enmeshed families) rather than those in which the members are less closely involved.

Systems in which the members have either a limited selection of alternatives (unskilled persons) or restricted opportunity to choose from the alternatives (economically dependent wives) are more subject to the tendency toward ordinality than are systems in which the members have many alternatives (skilled and competent experts) and the freedom to be selective (a financially independent single person). There are two other characteristics that strengthen the tendency toward ordinality. Formal systems tend to be affected more by precedents than informal systems and systems that are rigidly bound by rules are more subject to ordinality than families with fewer rules to maintain.

Kinds of Change

In this section we will use a previous way of thinking to synthesize the work of Dell and Watzlawick. This synthesis will help increase the understanding of family change by indicating some of the components of change. Our previous position[32] is that change is either structural (change within the system in that its organization remains continuous) or organizational (change that entails the destruction of the system). We will build on these ideas but, first, we must clarify the meaning of "continuity" and its reciprocal, "discontinuity."

"Continuity" is the idea that a system's behavior always mirrors precedents, that systemic behavior is consistent (of a piece) with that which previously occurred. Obviously, "discontinuity" is the opposite, the idea that behavior can dramatically change, that behavior can be separate from precedents. This is a restatement of the ordinality/equifinality discussion.

Thus there are two classifications of change: structural change/organizational change and continuous change/discontinuous change.[33] It is tempting to equate structural change with continuous change and make organizational change synonymous with discontinuous change. Unfortunately, the matter is more complicated. In order to encompass its complexity, we will first show how Dell and Watzlawick treat change and then we will attempt to clarify the matter by synthesizing their different perspectives.

Dell's ideas regarding change revolve around the idea of coherence. He indicates that continuous change shows coherence and that what we call "structural change" is the means by which a system maintains its organization. That is, with structural change, the parts fit together differently than they did before and so the organization can continue to exist, albeit with a different structure.

On the other hand, "discontinuous change" is synonymous with "organizational change" and the "disruption of the physical or behavioral coherence of the system" (Dell, 1982, p. 34). Dell maintains that discontinuous change always entails the prior death of the system, but also that "All multi-individual interactional systems are capable of true discontinuous change . . ." (1982, p. 34). Apparently, systems can change discontinuously, but the system's previous existence as a coherent unit must end in order for this drastic type of change to occur.

In the analysis of Watzlawick et al. (1974), structural change is called "first order change" and a change of the system is called a "second order change." This would seem to present no theoretical problems because we can equate first order change with structural change and second order change with organizational change. These analysts see discontinuous change as possible; they indicate that when a system changes discontinuously, it is "recalibrated." Its "setting"[34] is changed (p. 147). With the new setting,[35] either there are unprecedented ways of interacting and/or the system's personnel changes. Watzlawick et al. allow for the existence of a kind of discontinuous change that does *not* require the prior death of the system.

Putting the ideas of these two analysts together we get the following terminology. "Structural" "continuous" and "first order" change all refer to change within the system at the structural level. This change allows the system as a whole to maintain its basic character; system coherence is provided by revision of patterns at the subsystem level. We will refer to this kind of change as "structural change."

On the other hand, "organizational," "discontinuous," and "second order" change refer to a system's change in that the old system no longer exists and one or more new systems with different personnel, or with different ways of relating, and with different values is created. The new systems are not continuous with the system they have replaced; precedents from the former system do not significantly influence the new systems' interactions and transactions.

We would suggest that another kind of change be added: "first order discontinuous" change. This change would include dramatic and unprecedented changes that substantially affect the system's setting but do not destroy the system. In a "first order discontinuous change," the components change so that, although there is no organizational change, the system's activity or rules or personnel are apparently new. This newness is at the subsystem level and "newness" only refers to parts of the system. The system itself continues and most of its ways follow precedents.

An example should help clarify the matter. An organizational change occurs when a couple has a bitter argument that begins over some minor matter and escalates to such proportions that one person leaves the dyad and does not return. Clearly, the persons are no longer intimate and are not together; they are no longer organized as a family. The system as a family system has ceased to exist.

"Structural change" does not indicate such drastic change. An example of a structural change is the change in parenting that occurs as a child grows up. When a parent allows a child to have independence and responsibility commensurate with maturation, parent-child interaction changes but love, concern, and intimacy remain more or less steady, that is, continuous. Or, when family members decide that their financial well-being requires budgeting instead of uncontrolled expenditures and they begin to budget their money and thereby maintain their solvency, they have made a first order change. Their solvency has been maintained; the continuity of values and patterns exists. There is no organizational change.

The other kind of structural change, first order discontinuous change, is exemplified by a couple's increasing their family size. The people decide that their relationship is such that a new member should be brought into the family. With the birth, the family is still identifiable as a family (it is organizationally the same) but its personnel, rules, and activity are all dramatically revised. Structurally, there have been major changes and the continuity of interaction patterns may be difficult to see.

Another example of first order discontinuous change has to do with a change in structure without a change in family membership. A couple has a bitter argument, one of a series, and each decides that "we can't go on like this." They decide that, if they are to continue living together, they will have to rid themselves of contentious issues. Suppose that their problem centers around the wife's feeling that she has insufficient freedom and the husband's view that she is overly dependent and incapable of taking care of herself. When they reestablish their relationship, they do so on a new basis: that she take a job and be responsible for herself. His contribution would be to "get off her case" and stop belittling her efforts to "find herself." Let us further imagine that this change allows them to live together without periodic unresolved conflict. If this were to happen, their group's organization would be familial yet some of their interaction would be discontinuous with their former ways of relating.

Loops: Change, Stability, and Interaction Sequences

Thoroughness requires that we consider "loops," an important part of the family system view. Systems analysis has some of its roots in cybernetics and others in communication and information theory. An important component of these perspectives is the way that a system's patterns are corrected. In information theory, this correction has to do with the way that mismatched information is handled. Mismatched information is also known as "error" or "deviation" and refers to the existence of some discrepancy such as the difference between expectations and results or the difference between some projectile's position and the location of the bull's-eye. When there is some surprise like a missed goal or some misbehavior (another way of saying "behavior not congruent with expectations"), there is some attempt to correct the error. Basically, there are two different ways that deviation is handled in systems; these two ways are called negative feedback loops and positive feedback loops (Hoffman, 1971; Watzlawick et al., 1967; Muruyama, 1968).

It should be noted at the outset that the term "feedback" can be confusing because it has three different meanings. One is associated with family systems theory, the second with general systems theory, and the third has nothing specifically to do with systems. The family systems meaning of "feedback" has to do with its use in the terms "positive feedback loops" and "negative feedback loops." Inasmuch as these terms are explained below, we need only report here that both of these kinds of loops have to do with the family's method of dealing with behavior that is new or nonnormative. It is this meaning of the term that is used in this book.

The second use of "feedback" has to do with systems and information. When a system acts, it frequently receives information about how well it is behaving or how well it behaved. This particular kind of information—that is, information about the system's performance which comes to the system from outside—is called feedback. Some of this information might be evaluative and, if it is, it fits into the following category as well.

The third use of "feedback" is not specifically systemic and, when used this way, "feedback" is a synonym for "evaluation." This is the way that the term is used most commonly among the general public. If someone does not care for my performance they might tell me so and, if they do, I call that "negative feedback"; if the person tells me that he likes my work, I call that "positive feedback." It should be noted that "positive feedback" and "negative feedback" are different from "positive feedback loops" and "negative feedback loops."

Negative Feedback Loops

The term "negative feedback loops" is sometimes difficult to understand because it is confused with criticism (negative feedback) and because "negative" carries the connotation of adverse. As was pointed out, negative feedback loops have nothing to do with criticism. A negative feedback loop is an interaction sequence in which one part of the sequence negates the effect of another part of the sequence in such a way that the system remains unchanged. This will be recognized as a first order change, a change of structure with a negative feedback loop; change occurs at a lower level of family interaction in order that stability be preserved at a higher level.

Families that are stable have negative feedback loops that are very strong. The Spencers, for example, use negative feedback loops and we will consider two examples drawn from *Silver Anniversary*. In the argument between Mr. and Mrs. Spencer regarding the bad check, Mr. Spencer was angry, uttered harsh words, and the emotional space between Mr. and Mrs. Spencer increased. The system's emotional setting deviated from its normal position. The distance between Mr. and Mrs. Spencer became uncomfortable, Mrs. Spencer's symptoms warned Mr. Spencer of the onset of a crisis, Mrs. Spencer became coy, and Mr. Spencer relented as she won him over. The error, the increase in the emotional distance which is the first half of the negative feedback loop, was corrected; it was negated by the second half of the loop, Mrs. Spencer's archness and her appeal to his protectiveness. The system was unchanged.

Another example of a negative feedback loop concerns the script itself. If you believe that the better ending is the one in which Carolyn stays at home, you are calling for a negative feedback loop. The first part of the loop concerns the time when Carolyn left home and her leaving entailed the severing of some mutually contingent roles and the separation of family members. With the second ending and her staying at home, her eventual readmission to the family entails a second loop, one which negates the effect of the first until the feelings of separation are eradicated and the family members are close again.

Negative feedback loops have to do with information. That is, when information which is either behavioral (e.g., changed personal activity) or ideational (e.g., an idea that some family pattern no longer works) is introduced to the system, the components act in such a way as to minimize the effect of that information and to maintain the system's overall stability. The essence of the system—that is, the most basic values of its members, the interactional and transactional patterns that are associated with these values, its "working agreement"—is maintained by some low level adjustment that reduces the effect of the deviation.

The example above of the changing relationship of the parent and child so that the relationship maintains a relatively steady level of intimacy is a case in point. Over the years, a parent-child relationship will have its "ups and downs" and these variations in satisfaction have to do with differences in the parent's and child's definition of the nature of their relationship and attendant behavior. Commonly, a parent's and a child's level of satisfaction reflects the parent's flexibility in allowing the child to be independent, the child's acceptance of behavioral limitations, and each one's willingness to resolve without rancor their inevitable differences of opinion. When the child deviates from the established way of the family, the parent compromises in such a way that other family members' rights are maintained and the child experiences freedom commensurate with his maturity. The overall quality of the parent-child relationship thereby maintains its continuity and intimacy. The detrimental effect of the child's deviation has been negated.

Positive Feedback Loops

With positive feedback loops, the situation is quite different. Positive feedback processes amplify the error or deviation which inheres in some event until the continuity of the system is threatened. The particular event may be initially insignificant but the error involved is accentuated and "a mountain is made out of a molehill." Using the same example as in the previous paragraph, when the child deviates, the parent may become angry or upset. If this is met by rebellion on the child's part and the child's rebellion and the parent's restraint feed on each other in a vicious cycle, the previous level of intimacy will be upset. (If someone relents and parent and child resolve their differences, a negative feedback loop exists.) If the child leaves the home, a second order change will have occurred.

A positive feedback loop, then, is an interaction sequence without countervalence. Lacking a component that dampens escalation, the system explodes and dramatically changes (Watzlawick et al., 1967, p. 146, 158; Montgomery, 1981, pp. 83–85). In information terms, a positive feedback loop occurs when information regarding some deviation is managed in such a way that the deviation is amplified and, if unchecked, the loop results in a change of the system.

An example of a positive feedback loop which can be drawn from *Silver Anniversary* is the interaction sequence between Debbie and Carolyn. Their interaction started peacefully and then matters got out of hand. Both persons became spiteful, Carolyn's anger was fed by Debbie's dependence and Debbie's unhappiness fed on Carolyn's anger and there was an escalation of the intensity of feelings until Debbie left the kitchen and her leaving terminated the sequence. Debbie's leaving also destroyed their coalitional system and only time will tell if the destruction is permanent or temporary.

Understanding types of loops helps us to understand families. Consider the "here we go again" phenomenon (called "irresistible runs" by Hoffman, 1971, p. 301). Anyone who has lived in a family for even a short period of time can think of situations in which they have observed family interaction and have thought to themselves that they have experienced the interaction before. This thought, "here we go again," arises when the observer sees cues from one person being taken up by another. Further, the subsequent entanglement reminds the observer that this particular interaction sequence is virtually identical to others that they have previously witnessed. The sequence may be either joyous or conflictual but it is the conflictual kind, those that hurt, that bring out the dèjá vu feeling more strongly.

The "here we go again" phenomenon helps us to understand both positive and negative feedback loops. Conflict situations commonly follow a familiar pattern. When conflict is just beginning, it starts slowly as the two combatants get into position. They begin to test each other and if all systems are "go," so to speak, their interaction becomes more active and intense and each person's activity and intensity supports the agitated state of the other. This mutual escalation, this positive feedback loop, continues until one or both of the players comes to the realization that either their own safety or the continuation of the family is in jeopardy. At that point, the threatened person will stop the escalation (take a complementary one-down position) and the other, having no one to fight, will relent and the situation will eventually return to normal.

The process of achieving normalcy will include another positive feedback loop as one person's desire for better relations and stability meshes with the other's similar desire and they apologize and make up. The two positive feedback loops taken together constitute a negative feedback loop because the product of these two positive loops is an unchanged family. In situations in which the two positive feedback loops negate each other, family time reverts to "year zero" (Koestler, 1954), and the family will later go through a repeat of the same interaction sequence. To use the vernacular, family members fight and then make up; the situation returns to normal.

Commonly, positive feedback loops are not allowed to run their course. They only are allowed to go to the point where the situation gets close to "getting out of hand" (read, "where the situation threatens system continuity"). Then, instead of making an organizational change or a first order discontinuous change, the members defuse the situation and neither structure nor organization is affected. The issue, being unresolved, is "tabled" and is available for recall when a member "needs" a fight to vent anxiety or to satisfy some other need.

Organizational and first order discontinuous changes occur only when positive feedback loops go to their full extent.

Carolyn's exit of a year previous was, apparently, the culmination of a positive feedback loop that had existed over a period of years. When she left, the four-person system ended and that was the death of that four-person family organization.

However, the family continued as a triad and the new triad went through a time of difficulty as a new structure was put into place. The new structure provided for the needs of each of the three Spencers and otherwise fulfilled the family's organizational requirements. Therefore, it can be said that Carolyn's leaving destroyed the old four-person organization but a new triad grew up in its place and the new triad's structure resulted from a second order change.

It should be noted that an unrestrained positive feedback loop can contribute to a system's functioning if it promotes change when dramatic change is required. An example of an appropriately unrestrained positive feedback loop would be an escalating sequence that results in a change that brings about a new organization to replace one in which integration was produced by the belittlement of a family member.

This example promotes more optimism than examples drawn from *Silver Anniversary* because the Spencers underwent all kinds of change and yet never achieved family stability without personal belittlement. The Spencers' major structural problem was that the members tended to end positive feedback loops before a change could take place in the system. The result was a stable family but one in which stability was purchased with the loss of self. Each member was very good in bringing matters back to a state of normalcy but none was adept at promoting change to such an extent that their own growth-oriented needs were met and/or the system was changed.

AN ADAPTATION-BASED CLASSIFICATION OF FAMILIES

We have noted that families are all open to some degree and we have indicated that the relative openness of a system refers to the amount of information that comes into a system and the way that that information is managed. The family's next step is to deal with the meaning of the information, that is, either to adapt or not to adapt to what this information means about the effectiveness of family patterns. Families can be classified on the basis of *the way that they adapt to received information.*[36]

Family systems can be placed, according to Levant, in one of three categories, these categories being based on the kinds of feedback loops that predominate. He calls one type of family "homeostatic" as it is characterized primarily by negative feedback loops. Members in families so classified act both individually and in concert to minimize the effect of incoming information. Adaptation is usually such that former interaction and transaction patterns are reinforced. The families in this category exhibit pattern rigidity and a high degree of agreement as to goals, preferred interaction patterns, and desired structure. The tendency toward ordinality is in evidence. The Spencers give evidence of being a "homeostatic" family.

His second category includes "balanced-growth" family systems. Families in this category operate with a mixture of positive and negative feedback loops. The negative feedback loops encourage the system's stability in that they promote the continuity of former values, former interaction patterns, and structure. This promotes adaptation by providing a reason for pattern revision ("to maintain what we have"). Moreover, negative feedback loops provide the predictability and order which are prerequisites of the decision making and decision implementation that adaptation involves.

Positive feedback loops are important to balanced-growth families. These loops make it possible for able families to change their inappropriate patterns in response to information. For these families, pattern continuity is not as important as effective functioning. The existence of positive feedback loops insures that families will develop new ways of interacting and transacting.

The "balance" of balanced-growth systems refers to the use of a mixture of positive and negative feedback loops. The positive feedback loops promote change and balanced-growth systems are so well integrated (because of their active negative feedback loops) that members can let positive feedback loops escalate without becoming concerned about the family's disintegration. With both stability-enhancing and change-promoting mechanisms firmly in place, these families can adapt very well.

The third family category includes families identified as "random." Random systems are characterized by positive feedback loops and families in this category focus on the future without much consideration of the past. Random families appear to be characterized by unpredictable behavior as their emphasis on adaptation over continuity generates unprecedented interaction sequences.

As Levant indicates, families in each category can be classified as being ably functioning or poorly functioning. Families in the balanced-growth category are structurally sound and generally function well. When these families are dysfunctional, the dysfunction is to be found in some characteristic (such as incompatible deep values of husband and wife) other than their mix of positive and negative feedback loops.

Families in the homeostatic category function very ably from time to time; their ability to function depends upon their not being required to adapt to personal, relationship, or contextual change. Without being required to change, their emphasis on goal consensus, integration, stability, and pattern continuity generates peace, complacency, and satisfaction. Their reluctance to revise their patterns lowers their effectiveness when patterns are kept that no longer work.

Families typified as random are highly adaptive at the subsystem level; that is, the members are individually adaptive. Each member's adaptation provides the basis of the family's strength and if the family members are so compatible that the advancement of one member's goals promotes the success of other family members, families in the "random" category can work well. These families will also work satisfactorily if the means exist within the family to coordinate the members' adaptation. Families in this category run into difficulty when the means of coordinating the activities of the individual members is not present and when error or deviation that is introduced into the family is exacerbated in positive feedback loops and these loops upset the system's interaction and its structure.

Structurally, the balanced-growth families are the most sound and the other two types are functional if, in the case of homeostatic families, some positive feedback loops happen so that adaptation can occur and, in the case of random families, mutual goals are advanced and integration is thereby promoted. Homeostatic families work best when they allow for positive feedback loops and random families work best when they allow for some negative feedback loops. Obviously, this means that both the random type and the homeostatic types work best when they are most like the balanced-growth type of family.

This completes the consideration of system stability and change. The final section of this book has to do with the development of systems.

STAGES OF SYSTEM DEVELOPMENT

The development of a system has been considered by several theorists (Land & Kenneally, 1977; Bateson, 1979; Constantine, 1983; Speer, 1970; Maruyama, 1968). There is some consensus among theorists that systems change over time and that the stages are identifiable. We will consider two different theoretical approaches, that of Bateson and that of Land.

Bateson: Simple to Complex Transformation

Bateson writes that a system becomes "more simple" over time. By "more simple" he means that interaction becomes less confused and less chaotic, that interaction becomes more ordered and predictable. In writing about the play of a dog and gibbon, Bateson (1979) states that, "There has been an evolution of fitting together. With minimum change in dog or gibbon [as individual entities] the system dog-gibbon has become simpler—more internally integrated and consistent" (p. 152).

Paradoxically, what Bateson refers to as greater simplicity, others (Constantine, 1983; Speer, 1970) call greater complexity. Greater simplicity means that interaction becomes more ordered and behavior becomes more predictable. The order and predictability are engendered by the development of habitual and mutually understood behavior sequences. The system is simplified in that the participants know what can be expected in actions and interactions. Paradoxically, *increased order and predictability require increased complexity both in the coordination of mutual activities and in the integration of the group.* Shared expectations are associated with increasingly complicated structural arrangements.

The increased simplicity in interaction (greater predictability) which is the result of greater systemic complexity may become more understandable if you consider your own experience. If you reflect back on a significant relationship, one that lasted for a period of time, you will recall that in the beginning there was much *tentative* behavior. The tentativeness was the product of uncertainty as to how the other person would interpret your moves. At the same time, you were also attempting to understand the meaning of *her* behavior. With time and experience in interacting, it became easier to predict the behavior that was coming and the personality behind the behavior became better known and appeared to be more internally consistent. Then, instead of feeling awkward and tentative, you became more confident and certain and it became simpler to be a part of the relationship. Our point is that the simplicity was possible only because your *interaction sequences became patterned* and your behavior and your friend's behavior became *coordinated.* The patterning and coordination of interaction are components of structure.

Land and the Control/Influence/Sharing Transformation

As indicated earlier, Land and Kenneally (1977) stipulated that parts of systems provide stability but that systems themselves "grow." For Land, a system's growth is its increase in complexity as it creates more intricate interconnections both internally and transactionally.

Land states that a system develops (becomes more ordered and less chaotic) and passes through three stages, each one having a characteristic mode of structural interaction. In the first stage of system development, the system components attempt to *control* the behavior of other system components. This stage continues until the system's growth is limited by the members' control attempts. After a period of interstage disorganization, the second stage is entered and, in this stage, the components attempt to *influence* each other. Influence is associated with a new period of growth as the components are freed from either controlling or being controlled. Influence, in its turn, becomes growth-limiting and eventually gives way to *sharing* as the predominant characteristic of interaction. Finally, sharing leads to intrasystem sameness and the system becomes a unity with parts that are alike. Increased complexity can only come from the system's combining with some other system. When this combining occurs, a new system is born. With a new system, the process of control-influence-sharing is repeated (Land & Kenneally, 1977).

In other words, control is replaced by influence and influence is replaced by sharing as each of these interaction modes are explored, exhausted, and left behind. Sharing eventually becomes unsatisfactory when unanimity and order are attained and the system, now unified, begins to relate with some other contextual unit. This new relationship requires that new processes be developed to bring order out of chaos and these new processes are, in turn, control, influence, and sharing.

In family terms, at the beginning of a dyadic relationship, each person attempts to control the other's actions. Control is necessitated by the discomfort occasioned by nonpredictability. But, control does not conduce to intimacy in relationships and so, when more intimacy is desired, the lovers attempt to be subtler and they substitute influence for control. Influence, however, is eventually replaced by sharing when (and if) the lovers desire the intimacy that only sharing can provide.

Eventually, sharing runs its course; order and intrasystem sameness exist and the predictable becomes boring. New ways of interacting are sought. Since sharing is the identifying characteristic of the system at the top end of development, the system can only develop by an organizational change or a first order discontinuous change. These dramatic changes are exemplified by the birth of a child, a marital separation, or a new living arrangement with some other person or family. With changes such as these, a new system is developed and with this new system comes control, followed by influence, followed by sharing.

Summarizing System Development

Living systems in general and family systems in particular change over time. Although we have suggested that some stages can be named, sober reflection indicates that our knowledge is such that only the existence of developmental processes can be stipulated, that the naming of stages is premature. It is safe to say, however, that processes of a developing system have the following characteristics:

interaction among the members becomes more general, more all-encompassing;

interaction among the members touches each person more deeply;

interaction becomes more intense and if the system is a family intimacy develops;

greater member interdependency develops;

bonds are established, there exists more shared commitment, more shared identity;

precedents take on greater importance, there exists more continuity with the past;

predictability replaces randomness as the characteristic mode of interaction;

systems become more ordered, more sequences are repeated;

there is a greater need for the coordination of activities;

there is greater differentiation of the system from its context;

there is less internal differentiation;

with age, there is greater disorganization of the system's physical components.

All of these characteristics of a developing relationship involve the revision of patterns which, in turn, are created, maintained, and left behind as the system develops. It is exactly this process of creation, stability, and change which we have explored and endeavored to clarify.

In order to summarize the theory that has been presented and to put the theory in a concise form, we will present a model which includes what has been presented as well as that which follows in the glossary.

NOTES

30. "One-up" and "one-down" are descriptive, not evaluative terms. They describe the persons' places in the relationship's structure; they evaluate neither the positions nor the qualities of persons in these positions.

31. This is not to say that the well-being of all systems is either important or "good." Clearly, a family system which is integrated and coordinated but is based on the destruction of some members' growth or health should be improved or destroyed.

32. See above: *"What Changes, What is Unchanging."*

33. It should be remembered that structural change is a change at the subsystem level which allows the system to maintain its more basic and essential patterns. With an organizational change, however, the system itself ceases to exist and new and discontinuous systems are organized.

34. The recalibration of a system is exemplified by the changing of a setting on a thermostat. When the thermostat's setting is changed, the parts of the system, although identical, relate to each other in a different way. In a family, resetting would occur if a child were no longer

scapegoated and the mother and father attempted to solve their problems without triangulating the child.

35. "Setting" is not a good word to use in systems analysis because it has two different meanings; one concerns the family's internal processes (the internal calibration of the system) and the other its transactions (where a scene is "set"). In the first usage, "setting" and "calibration" are synonymous, and in the second, "setting" is synonymous with context. In this book, "setting" means the same as "calibration"; when we speak of context or environment, we will not use "setting."

36. Levant (1984) has done well in combining a number of different family classification schemes and in eliminating the confusion associated with mixing information management with family adaptation. We borrow from his perceptive analysis (pp. 13—16) and add to it. We use his typology which includes the term "homeostatic" even though we find his use of this term objectionable.

Chapter 5

THE MODEL

In this chapter, we have attempted to put together in a
different way the ideas that have been explained previously.
This different method is developmental in approach since it
begins with the formation of the family unit and, in turn,
discusses the nature of coupling, the system's separating from
nonmember contextual elements, and special issues such as
change and stability. Since much of family interaction concerns intimacy and its counterpart conflict, these terms are
also briefly explored.

    I. Preceding the establishment of any particular family
       system,
        A. There exists an ongoing context, a social system
           that prescribes what constitutes a family's func-
           tions.
        B. Subsequent to providing the medium for the
           development of the dyadic relationship, the so-
           cial system undergoes constant structural change
           and this change continues to perturb any dyads
           that are formed.

C. Within this changing social context, there are two independent, structurally determined, and mindful person systems. Each one of these persons is coupled to the social structure in an idiosyncratic fashion, the idiosyncrasies derive from the way each person defines the world as this results from his interpretation of his experience, his unique socialization, his pattern of group membership, etc. Each person continues to be uniquely connected with his context;

II. The two persons meet and

A. With meeting and subsequent interaction, if their structures are compatible, each person system perturbs the other (and is perturbed by the other) and their lives take on a mutual contingency. There is a fit of structures and behavior-in-interaction. They become structurally coupled as each one's structural requirements mesh with the structural requirements of the other. Each person's structural plasticity allows for continued coupling (interdependence).

Structural coupling, compatibility, matching, perturbation are terms which have to do, in family systems, with intimacy and the perception on each person's part that needs are being met. Each person is "loved" in ways that make sense to him and mutually contingent, intimate role careers (acquaintance, friend, partner, lover) are established.

With interaction,

1. Patterns emerge. Patterns are the product of process (actions are repeated, they fit with another person's actions, interaction sequences become redundant, patterns are established).

2. The dyad has characteristics not found in either person (emergence, holism, synergy).

    3. The resulting system has unique characteristics (equifinality).

    4. Complementary and/or symmetrical aspects of the relationship take shape; patterns of togetherness/separateness, responsiveness/aloofness, etc., become established.

  B. Each person system retains its coherence with its former structural states and the ordinal tendency is relevant for each person.

    1. Family formation proceeds slowly, allowing time for personal adaptation.

    2. Conflict is to be expected as personal coherence will sometimes be incompatible with dyadic development.

    3. Each person (somewhat independently) changes his structure as they adapt to non-dyadic perturbations.

III. The two-person system becomes a family system if certain organizational requirements are met:

  A. Interaction is characterized by intimacy or attempts to gain intimacy.

  B. Other conditions which allow for organizational development are met:

    1. Each person is free from other commitments so that continuing intimate interaction can occur.

    2. Gender and age (and other characteristics such as appearance, family acceptance, social class, religion, religiosity) are consistent with social/personal prescriptions.

IV. The formation of a family system is promoted by:

  A. The tendency (general for all systems) of each person to grow.

    1. When needs are met, the meeting of deeper needs is attempted.

    2. The goodness of fit of the persons' structures encourages automatic behavior and this frees the conscious mind so that it can solve other problems.

       3. Other relationship escalators (changed future plans, couple identity, others' expectations) are influential.

       4. The persons allow their systems to become joined in increasingly more complex ways.

  B. There is development along the control-manipulation-sharing pattern.

  C. Systemic interaction becomes more predictable, more routine, more structured.

V. The emerging family system continues to relate to other parts of its context:

  A. The dyad becomes differentiated (separate but connected) from its context.

  B. By whatever name, "information," "triggers," "perturbations" occur and persons in the family interpret these phenomenon, reach a working agreement, and each person transacts with external institutions and groups on the basis of his understanding of the agreement.

  C. Structural coupling occurs when the family system is mutually perturbable with external systems (other groups and institutions)

  D. Related to (or another way of considering) the patterns of transactional perturbations is the placement of the family on the closed-open continuum.

IV. The system also develops internally:

  A. An idiosyncratic structure becomes established and this structure is associated with adaptation and stability. First, *stability:*

      1. The system's stability is observed as being a function of:

          a. *Its setting.* The persons in the family become uncomfortable when other family members interact with them in unprecedented ways. Each member attempts to reduce this discomfort and often the reduction is attempted by the reestablishment of former patterns.

From this activity of change and counterchange, it appears that the family has characteristic settings.

b. *The ordinal tendency.* A family's patterns appear to exist over time and the continuing interactional and transactional structures provide continuity.

   i. Precedents tend to be extended through time and effective structure is reinforced by success. Ineffective structure is sometimes continued when the ineffectiveness is *unevenly* felt by family members, when habit is strong, and when family members fail to perceive pattern ineffectiveness.

   ii. Families can adapt to perturbations in a number of ways and one way is by first order continuous change. This type of change is provided by negative feedback loops.

   iii. First order change can also promote system stability even though the new patterns appear to be unprecedented. This is "first order discontinuous" change. Despite the appearance of discontinuity, the new patterns must fit with the system's existing structure.

c. *Integration:* Since parts of the family system can exist independently, the maintenance of the system is problematic and requires the establishment and maintenance of bonds.

d. Coalitions are formed and these further stability by providing a "common front" for those in the coalition and thus give strength to those resisting change.

     e. Communication patterns promote stability as when they allow for differences to be resolved.

     f. The family system being closed as to information flow: Information can be unsensed (missed) and/or managed in order to minimize the need for change.

     g. *Coherence:* Each subsystem attempts to maximize itself and maintain its own coherence; this implies the minimization of others' change. Subsystem interaction maintains the coherence of the system.

     h. *Its working agreement:* The working agreement allows the family to remain stable in the face of disagreement.

2. There is adaptation, change in the family system's structure.

     a. A family system develops:

          i. As it adapts to its interpretations of contextual change, of change in members, and changes in interaction among members.

          ii. To the degree that it is an open system with information accurately sensed, generously shared, and accepted.

     b. Disintegration is also a fact of family life.

          i. Administrative failure sometimes occurs and the family's activities are not coordinated; there may be subsystem aggrandizement; and (rarely) the family may destroy the context on which it depends.

          ii. The "entropy law" holds that the physical parts of systems always wither away.

B. A system's organization is stable at times and at other times subject to change.

1. Organizational stability is provided:
   a. At the subsystem level by the system's parts countervailing against change in each other.
   b. By structural stability, which encourages organizational stability by enabling the system to perform its prescribed functions for both society and for family members. There can be no organization without effective structure.
2. Change is a system level activity and
   a. As we have seen above (III and IV), a system develops and its interaction and transaction patterns become more complex.
   b. At the same time, systems tend toward disorganization; both system death and the subsequent renewal of other systems (either brand-new or reconstituted) are to be expected.
      i. Dysfunction occurs when the system fails to fulfill its functions.
      ii. Discontinuous change is perceived as occurring when parts of the old system are either no longer joined or are joined in ways that no longer serve to fulfill their former functions. That is, the family's parts are joined in such a way that intimacy needs are not met.
      iii. Organizational change occurs by means of positive feedback loops. These maximize deviance and continue to escalate until the organization of the system (separation of parts, dysfunction) is affected.

V. Intimacy
   A. The components of intimacy:
      1. A relationship of duration
      2. Being known
      3. Being seen as a whole person
      4. Surrender of self without feelings of being used
      5. Trust and trustworthiness
      6. A sense of belonging
   B. Intimacy is a species-specific need
   C. Family is major provider of intimacy
   D. Sources of intimacy
      1. Sexual interaction: indicates the progress of increasing intimacy and escalates intimacy
      2. Being affirmed
         a. Being loved supports a person's feeling of worthiness
         b. Being in agreement about interaction basics: togetherness (close or distant), relationship structure (chaotic, loose, rigid), roles (free or stereotypical), communication (disclosive or secretive)
         c. Reaching agreement or agreeing to disagree
         d. Spontaneity
   E. Family systems are different from other systems because of the centrality of intimacy. Usually, families in contemporary society are entered into to obtain intimacy and, as a result, that which happens in families affects intimacy, or is seen in terms of the way that it affects intimacy.
   F. Intimacy is not constant and the level varies from relationship to relationship and varies over time in the same relationship. The basis of intimacy also varies both across (e.g., passion to partnership to deep understanding) and within relationships. Not uncommonly, intimacy lessens and ceases to serve as the reason for staying

together but, instead is turned on and off in order that the family can stay together.

VI. Conflict

A. Conflict is defined as an interaction sequence characterized by the participants' discomfort and the use of disagreement to lessen the feelings of discomfort. The components of conflict, then, are:

1. Feelings of discomfort

   a. Sources of discomfort can be personal (aging), familial (dashed expectations), transactional (one's unemployment), social (change in cultural values)

   b. Sources of discomfort can be general and free floating (unhappiness) or specific (disagreement about parenting)

2. An ideology that conflict is an acceptable way to reduce discomfort.

3. Another person who is uncomfortable or whose discomfort can be triggered.

B. The uses of conflict, which can exist singly or in combination:

1. To reduce discomfort.

2. To reinforce male superiority and female subjugation.

3. To satisfy needs associated with the abuser's mental disorder.

4. To increase space in relationship.

5. To make the relationship personally and/ or mutually more satisfying.

C. Conflict is to be expected in intimate relationships due to a relationship's intensity, importance, and the changes in persons, in relationships, and in context.

D. Different dimensions of conflict:

1. Constructive (deals directly with source of discomfort) or destructive (lessens discomfort, at least temporarily, without affecting source)

2. Complementary:
   a. Associated with the intensification of complementariness
   b. Stopped with evidence of symmetry ("Let's both be more sharing"; "Okay.")

3. Symmetrical:
   a. Associated with escalation
   b. Stopped with evidence of complementariness ("Yes, you're right.")

4. Conflict in an unrestrained positive feedback loop leads to structural or organizational change; most conflict is stopped prior to such change and negative feedback loops occur and systemic stability results.

5. Conflict can be overt and explicit or covert and hidden.

6. People engage in conflict over many things (or none) and the topic may have nothing to do with the use of conflict (see B. above). For example, the topic of conflict (such as money, sex, parenting) is usually only *the medium through which* discomfort is assuaged.

D. Since conflict cannot be avoided, it should be managed by making it constructive, non-repeated (one conflict per topic), overt/explicit, relative to the topic being worked through, and subject to rules associated with dignity, honesty, clear expression, and the enhancement of intimacy.

CONCLUSION

As was noted at the outset, the major goal of social science is to help us to understand the way that people act. Of course, "understanding human behavior" is too large an undertaking for a single work and the effort has been limited here to the consideration of family-related behavior. Even this was too broad an area of inquiry; so the focus on families has been through the narrower lens of the system's perspective. We also attempted to widen our focus by synthesizing systems ideas with ideas from other sources. In looking at families in this way, we found theory to be at times helpful, and also to adduce terminological ambiguity. We attempted to use the theory where it helped us to understand family-related behavior, and where we found a lack of clarity we attempted to lessen ambiguity.

The reader, who is the judge of the success of these efforts, may wish to consider his own family life in the light of this analysis and decide how well the theory fits with real-life family experience.

GLOSSARY

Adaptation. The processes associated with family members' altering their patterns in an attempt to improve functioning and integration given changes in a member, in members' relationships, and in the family's context. Adaptation occurs after a working agreement has been reached regarding the necessity of pattern revision.

Autonomy. The property of a minded system which enables it to adapt to potential influences in ways that reflect its own internal structure.

Boundaries. Inasmuch as "boundary" has long been an important systems term, we were loathe to omit it from this work. In justification of this omission: (1) "Boundary" is too general and its use is frequently ambiguous, (2) it is commonly reified, and (3) it tends to encourage a false view of a family's transactions.

The reason "boundary" is *ambiguous* in that it has too many meanings. Although "boundary" is ostensibly used to refer to information exchange, it has also been used to refer to the family's internal processes as it adapts to the information. A current example is: "Systems that have the same characteristics and the same boundaries over a long period of time remain in static equilibrium. These systems can be called closed because they do not adapt to changes in the outside environment" (Giles-Sims, 1983, p. 10). This author has included elements of adaptation in "boundary." We believe that clarity is advanced if a distinction is made between information and the family's subsequent *handling* of the information. We use "openness" to refer to the families' level of receptivity and "adaptation" to refer to their subsequent activity as they act on that information.

Other meanings of the term "boundary" can be handled more precisely with other words. "Membership" can be used to refer to the persons in the family and "coalitions" can be used to refer to groupings of family members.[37] "Information transmission" can be used to refer to what is called "boundary permeability" and "openness" can be used to refer to a system's receptivity. With its meanings defined more precisely by other words, "boundary" loses its value.

Reification of boundary has become common. Family theorists and researchers tend to forget that "boundary" is an abstract term and manipulate the label as if "boundaries" existed in a concrete way. Boundaries are now used as *explanations* of family phenomena (Boss & Greenberg, 1984).

Finally, the last reason to dispense with "boundary" is because it conduces us to think not how a system and its context are inextricably combined, but how they are separate. "Boundary" emphasizes transactional differentiation rather than the way the system fits with other contextual elements. Systems are only arbitrarily separated from each other for purposes of analysis; they are never·*as* separate as "boundary" implies. As Wilson put it:

> . . . when we reflect on it we find it hard to say
> with precision where the boundaries lie separating
> us as concrete individuals from the physical and the

> biological realms, to say nothing of the social. When
> are the air we breathe, the light and sound waves
> impinging on us—when are these us, and when non-
> us? Or the food we ingest and excrete—when is it
> us and when non-us? If there is some problem in
> asserting a clearly bounded identity here, how much
> more so is it to be expected in the realm of human
> interchange. (1966, p. 93)

It is true of families as well, this idea of fusion and interinvolvement. Whatever it is that is meant by "social life" or "society" or "culture" or the "human experience," we are all a part of it and the systemic emphasis on this essential unity is important. The use of "boundary," inasmuch as it minimizes this essential unity, leads to a faulty view of reality.

Calibration.   Being a term used in reference to the specification of physical properties, calibration is not acceptable for family theory. It is replaced by "setting" (Haley, 1963). See below.

Causation.   The idea that some entity's action is the result of either its antecedents or of forces that act contemporaneously upon it. As carried over from the physical sciences, the idea of causation precludes the possibility of the system's making a choice or otherwise acting on its interpretation of the information that it has received. "Cause" (of either the linear of multicausality type) does not belong in the systems lexicon. Mutual causality is not as easily rejected. Also known as "circular causality," mutual causality is the idea that each part of a system is interdependent with every other part. The intrasystemic meshing is so complete that "any delineation of before and after, or cause and effect is purely arbitrary" (Nichols, 1984, p. 128). Terminological purists such as Dell (1982) believe that the "causality" part of this term makes it inappropriate for systems; others use the term and emphasize the systemic quality of "mutual."

Change.   Used by some observers to refer to an event, behavior, or interaction eliciting their surprise; change is that which is contrary to an observer's expectations. When the change is in a family's established patterns, it is called "family change." The terms "social change," "contextual change," and "personal change" indicate perceived differences in prominent characteristics of, respectively, society, the system's context, and individuals. Clarity requires that change never stand alone; exactly that which is being described *as changing* should be made clear.

Coalition. A family subsystem that includes two or more family members and excludes at least one other member. Coalitions can either promote family effectiveness (generational coalitions) or they can tend to be dysfunctional (a cross-generational and/or gender-based coalition).

Closed system. A system that receives little information from either its context or its components. The less information that a system receives or the less information that is made available to trigger adaptation, the more defineable the system is as closed. No system, however, is *completely* closed.

Openness and closure are two ends of a continuum and the more open a system, the less closed it is and vice versa. Openness and closure refer to information being sensed by a family member, the exchange of that information, and the negotiation of the meaning of the information. Resulting interaction and transaction patterns are "adaptation"—not "openness."

Coherence. The idea that individual behavior patterns and family interaction patterns are continuations of *former* patterns. Patterns evolve, yet are always congruent with former patterns (Dell, 1982).

Cohesion. In early writing on the circumplex model, "cohesion" commonly subsumes the contradictory ideas of "integration" and (personal) "autonomy" (Olson & McCubbin, 1982, p. 48). In Olson, Russell, and Sprenkle's (1983) more recent work, "autonomy" is *not* included in the concept of cohesion. It seems to be advantageous, for purposes of specificity and clarity, to separate these two components, define them, and thereby eliminate "cohesion."

Communication.   The interpersonal negotiation of the meaning of some object, person, relationship, or situation.

Complementary relationships.   Relationships or parts of relationships based on the interactors' differences. "Complementarity" refers to a particular type of interpersonal fit, one in which behaviors fit due to their being opposites. An example is mother-child complementarity.

Components.   Parts of systems.

Conflict.   In families, conflict is an interaction sequence characterized by discomfort and the use of disagreement to lessen that discomfort.

Consensus.   Usually thought of as being a "meeting of the minds" and the basis of concerted action. As such, the term is misleading, since consensus can be reached by processes characterized by coercion, acquiescence, compliance, open sharing, or the manipulation of rewards. These processes affect each person's commitment to the decision, and the degree to which there will be harmony in the subsequent concerted action. "Working agreement," because it does not carry this same confusion, would be a good replacement.

Context.   The system's environment. Usually "context" refers to the next larger system of which the system under consideration is a part. Every system attempts to grow within its context: persons in their family context; families in society.

Continuity.   A system's pattern-consistency over time.

Cybernetics.   "Cybernetics is a term coined by Norbert Weiner (1948) to describe systems which regulate themselves by means of feedback loops. The basic elements in a cybernetic system are a receptor, a center and effector, and a feedback loop. Stimuli (or information) are received by the receptor and transmitted to the center, which reacts to the message and amplifies its signal. The message is then carried to the effector which reacts by discharging an output. The output is monitored by a feedback loop to the receptor which enables it to modify subsequent responses" (Nichols, 1984, p. 128). Nichols goes on to indicate, drawing on von Bertalanffy's ideas, that the cybernetic model is inadequate for humans because its mechanistic elements do not allow for human creativity, activity, or ". . . perceptual selection and cognitive structuring of their [humans'] sensory input" (p. 129).

Definition of the situation. Living systems confront reality through their senses and their subsequent behavior reflects their interpretation of the sensory information that was received. A minded system interprets (defines) the situation in terms of its genetic endowment, its past experience, and its aspirations, and behavior reflects a decision based on both conscious analysis of costs and benefits, and on unconscious needs.

Determinism. The idea, borrowed from the physical sciences, that behavior results from antecedents; that humans have no choices. "Determinism is the view that everything occurs lawfully. That is, for any event there is a set of laws or regularities connecting it with other events. With respect to human conduct, this implies, first, that there are circumstances—in our constitutions, background, environment, and character—that are jointly sufficient conditions for our behavior, including the choices that we make. It implies, second, that these choices in turn have causal consequences" (Brodbeck 1968, p. 671). We reject the idea of determinism when applied to human beings.

Disintegration. The "break up" of a system so that the parts are no longer a unified whole. In family systems, disintegration attends organizational change and the parts of the former family system are no longer "a family."

Disorganization. A system's state which is characterized by an inability to accomplish what must be accomplished if the system is to continue as a particular kind of organization. When a family's patterns are such that social functions and personal needs are not being met, the family can be described as disorganized. Disorganization sometimes leads to a system's disintegration.

Development. Changes in a system over time as the system adapts to internal changes and to its interpretation of contextual changes.

Dualism. The division of a unified entity into two separate parts which are then perceived to operate independently of each other.   Dualisms destroy the unit's essential whole-ness.   In the analysis of family systems, a dualism occurs when a member is analytically removed from the family and the behavior of the member is seen as being a cause or effect of family-level interaction.

Energy.   "Energy" has a specific physical science meaning which has to do with the ability of a system to do work, or to move objects at a rate that includes time and distance. This meaning of "energy" applies to the physical parts of systems and has reference to processes such as the body's ability to draw on resources and thereby be able to act.

One of the major differences between minded and nonliving systems is that the former's mental processes may direct the intake and expenditure of energy, while in the latter, energy usage is independent of any con-scious/unconscious thoughts.   "Energy," because its phys-ical science meaning does not include consideration of the system's will, depreciates this essential characteristic of living systems.   This minimization occurs when the word is used either vaguely to refer to living systems in general ("he has a lot of energy") or when it is specifically applied to the minded elements of living systems ("infor-mation is energy.")   To reduce confusion and to empha-size the minded components of living systems, it would seem to be advantageous to use the following synonyms: "strength" and the "capacity to act"; "level of activity" and "ability and willingness to act"; and "information" and "news of difference" instead of "energy" when it is these specific ideas that are meant.

Enmeshed.   A label commonly applied to families whose mem-bers have a low level of differentiation from each other. That is, the members are so mutually involved that each has a strong family identity and little personal identity. "Enmeshed families" function poorly at times because the members' sensitivity to each other's feelings and moods encourages *all* members to get disorganized or upset or dysfunctional when one member gets upset.   Although families can be called "enmeshed," clear understanding is advanced if it is remembered that "enmeshment" is only a label, that enmeshment is not uniform within a family at any time, and that the level of enmeshment varies over time. Care should be exercised to avoid re-ification ("a typical enmeshed family").

Entropy. A physical science term that refers to the physical aspects of living systems and the tendency for these phys-ical parts to deteriorate, to become disordered, and to disappear.

Emergence. The idea that the whole is greater than the sum of the parts. A system is more than an aggregate of its parts for the reason that when parts combine they produce a unified whole with characteristics that cannot be found in the components as separate units. The existence of system properties that cannot be found in the system's parts was called "synergy" by Benedict (see Hampden-Turner, 1981), "non-summativity" by Watzlawick et al. (1967), and "holism."

Epistemology. A branch of science (the study of the way that organisms know, think, and decide) combined with a branch of philosophy (the study of the necessary limits and other characteristics of knowing, etc.) (Bateson, 1979). "Epis-temology" in this book means "the person's structure of knowledge and thought that directs his perceptions, his management of information, and his subsequent activi-ties."

Equifinality. The idea that the state of a system at any time is not necessarily established by its initial composition, properties, or membership. The more open a system is, the stronger is the tendency toward equifinality.

Family mind. Like "family goal" and "family paradigm," "family mind" has to do with the idea that "lengthy, intimate, relationships [can only] go forward [if there exists] a reconciliation integration, and shared develop-ment of . . . personal theories" (Reiss & Oliveri, 1980, p. 434). "Family mind" is the name given to the agree-ment.

   While it is reasonable to believe that family members must agree at some (as yet undetermined) level if the family is to continue and be intimate, it is also true that a family's consensus can never be such that transpersonal unity of thought can be reached and maintained or that some family-level consciousness can ever exist. Ideas such as "family mind" promote the perception of both this unity and this kind of group consciousness and, because they do, they restrict efforts to ascertain the ways that families deal with dissensus.

Because of this problem, and because "family mind" posits a subsystem characteristic at a system level, this term as well as "family goal" and "family paradigm" should be discontinued.

Family system.   A socially, legally, or internally identifiable human system organized to be long lasting, to fulfill certain functions for society (e.g., childbearing, socialization of young, sanction sexual intercourse), and to meet members' needs (e.g., intimacy).

Feedback.   Information about a system's performance that comes to the system from outside. "Feedback" is not to be confused with either "negative feedback loop" or "positive feedback loop," both of which are defined below.

First order change.   A pattern change at the structural level that allows the system as a whole to maintain stability, deep value consistency, and organizational integrity. In "first order continuous change," patterns that exist after the change are an extension of preceding patterns; in "first order discontinuous change," the resulting patterns are innovative and seemingly unrelated to precedents; they must, however, fit with significant elements of the system's structure.

Fit.   A deceptively simple term meaning that, in a system, all behavior meshes. By using "fit" rather than "cause," no assumption of sequence or relative influence is made; one person's behavior fits with another's behavior; "cause" is not considered (Dell, 1980).

General systems theory.   A perception of reality, pioneered by von Bertalanffy, that attempts to make sense out of the biological world, not by looking for cause and effect, isolating variables, nor reducing nature to its simplest units of being/activity; but by emphasizing the emergent qualities of interdependent living things, investigating the effect of context and function on the organization of these living things, and inquiring into how the parts of living systems combine themselves. General systems theorists attempt to find the essential qualities that are characteristic of all "information," "process," "integration," "change," and "structure."

Growth. The tendency of living systems to become interactionally and transactionally more complex (Land & Kenneally, 1977); a system's tendency to be more richly joined.

Holism. See "emergence."

Homeostasis. A popular system term referring to a system's tendency to maintain a steady state.

Although systems analysts from Watzlawick et al. (1967, p. 146) to Dell (1982) have indicated the ambiguity of this term, it has continued to be used as though its meaning were clear. At present, the use of "homeostasis" is neither necessary nor warranted.

Other words (stability, negative feedback loops) indicate with more clarity and specificity the many ideas covered by "homeostasis." Other ideas (that stability is maintained by subsystems while development is a system activity) more accurately specify the processes that have been lumped together and called "homeostasis."

Information. News of some difference or of some change an observer defines as being important (Bateson, 1979).

Information exchange. Information exchange is the generous and accurate expression and reception of news; it is the property of an individual or of individuals.

Information management. The management of information includes the exchange of information, the withholding of information, and the distribution of distorted information. Although affected by family properties, information management is a person's property.

Integration. A family's (or some other system's) degree of oneness; the strength of its bonds.

Interaction. Mutually contingent behavior of one system component with another system component. Family interaction includes all intrafamilial communication and relationships.

Interdependence. The idea that each person's family related behavior is associated with, depends upon, and fits with the family behavior of every other family member.

Intimacy. Strong positive feelings that have their source in interaction processes characterized by positive emotional attachment, general acceptance, persons being seen as wholes rather than as players of roles, high levels of trust, and a willingness to give without a sense of loss.

Living systems. Systems that can receive information and adapt to it. Examples of living systems are insects, trees, persons, families, universities, and creatures with a pair of ragged claws scuttling across the floors of silent seas (T. S. Eliot).

Levels. All systems are composed of parts, and (1) the parts, (2) the combinations of parts, and (3) the whole system comprise a logical hierarchy. The parts are always more simple than are the combinations of parts because higher order combinations must take into account the internal structure of the lower order components as well as providing for the fit between the components as entities in themselves.

Mind. Where consciousness, thought, volition, and feelings have their source; that which processes information.

Mindful. Having the ability to manage information, or to interpret and adapt to perturbations. Mindful is synonymous with minded.

Negative feedback loop. A way of handling deviation within a system so that the deviation is minimized and the organization of the system is not affected.

Non-summativity. See "emergence."

Open system. A system's degree of openness has to do with its propensity to receive information. Relative openness is a system's level of receptivity to information in comparison with some other system. "Openness" includes elements of "acquisition" (the active seeking of information or "curiosity") and "sensitivity" (the ability to decode sensate signals). See "closed system."

Organization. The way a group is established to meet its own system requisites and to fulfill societal expectations as these requisites and expectations are prescribed in a particular culture. "Organization" is specific to the system's particular socially defined function.

Ordinality or Ordinal Tendency. The tendency of a system to be affected by its initial membership, composition, and attributes. The more a system is "closed," the more powerful will be the tendency of ordinality.

Paradigm. A view or model of reality. The set of fundamental assumptions which are the basis for the person's world-taken-for-granted.

Patterns. The name given to a system's typical ways, its repeated interaction and transaction sequences.

Perturbation. Some change which is sensed by a system and interpreted. The system responds to its interpretation of the initial change and not directly to the change. The system's response is determined by its structure and not by the perturbation.

Phenomenologist. A social scientist who considers the thoughts and feelings of the persons being studied to be an important part of his inquiry.

Positive feedback loop. A way of handling deviation in a system such that deviation is amplified and the amplification tends toward organizational change.

Process. What is "going on" (Laing & Esterson, p. 22) in families. The means used to attain need satisfaction and meet organizational requirements.

Properties. Attributes or qualities of a system or some system component.

Punctuation. The non-systemic, arbitrary, and simplistic segmenting of a continuing and complex interaction sequence in such a way that a beginning of the sequence is posited and "cause" and "effect" elements are arbitrarily assigned.

Redundant. An adjective which is synonymous with "repeated."

Reification. The identification and naming of a phenomenon and the subsequent use of the label as an explanation. Reification abounds in social science and "mid-life crisis," "enmeshed," and "social class," are three examples of names that have been used as explanations for behavior.

Second order change. A system's organizational change which is of such magnitude that the former system ceases to exist and a new system (or systems) with a different membership and different patterns replaces it.

Setting. A family's patterns vary around some point which the members find comfortable. The setting is the accepted center point. Personal discomfort attends behavior and interaction that deviate too much from the accepted center; members attempt to reestablish the family's typical conduct and thereby reduce their discomfort.

Stability. The constancy of patterns, especially interactional patterns. A system's constancy is maintained by subsystem coherence.

Structure. Within an organization (specified by culturally prescribed functions) an idiosyncratic arrangement of parts (and relations between parts) develops (Maturana, 1978). In family systems, structure consists of a family's unique patterns as its patterns develop from attempts to meet members' needs and to fulfill the family's organizational requirements.

Structurally coupled. Two systems mutually perturb each other.

Structure-determined. The idea that what happens in a system when it is perturbed is determined by the system's structure rather than by the perturbing event (Dell, 1982).

Subsystem. An arbitrarily sectioned portion of a larger system.

Symmetrical relationships. These relationships are typified by equality; they are characterized by the interactors' desire for similarity. Interaction is based on the desire to be the same as the other and, frequently, there is a high level of competition between the participants.

Synergy. See "emergence."

System. A collection of interrelated components and the existing relationships between those components.

Transaction. Mutually contingent behavior of a system component with a nonsystem entity.

Triangulation. Triangulation is the process of establishing triadic interaction so that two persons are allied against a third.

Trigger. Something that perturbs a system; a contextual change to which the system adapts.

Working agreement. A sort of compromise that occurs because unanimity is not possible and dissolution over the issue is an inappropriate or unacceptable response. "Working agreement" only means that family members acknowledge that a particular definition will be used. The "agreement" part of "working agreement" refers to each member's agreement to use the definition; it does not indicate agreement with the definition itself. Each member agrees to act in a way that is acceptable to self and others but the agreed-upon way is not all the members' (or perhaps any member's) *first* choice.

The terms in the glossary can be placed in three categories. Words to be avoided are placed in the first category. These words are not included on Table 5-I. Words in this category include boundary, calibration, words having to do with cause-and-effect thinking, cohesion, determinism, family mind, homeostasis, energy, and other words such as stress and power which carry physical science connotations. Unhelpful mental activities such as punctuation and reification are also included in this first category and excluded from Table 5-I.

The second category includes systems theory terms too general to be useful when applied to families. System, living system, emergence, entropy, stability, change, and process are important systems terms but, when applied to families, require greater specification if they are to be useful. Such general systems terms are found in the first column of Table 5-I and the ideas they represent are specified in the other two columns.

In the third category are terms that are more specific in that they refer to minded systems (and are found in the second column) or family systems (found in the third column).

In Table 5-I, each horizontal section contains words that express a particular idea. In the first column, the idea is expressed in a general systems term, in the second column, the same idea is expressed in words relevant to minded systems, and in the third column, the idea is expressed in family-related terminology.

Table 5-I. Specification of Terms as to Level of Analysis

General terms	Minded systems terms	Family term
Change	Equifinality	Family development
	Adaptation	Information exchange/
	Autonomy	management
	Growth	Structure determined
		Second order change, positive feedback loops
	Trigger	Stressor
Structure	Fit	Interaction, complementary/symmetrical
	Interdependence	Enmeshed, triangulate
Organization	Function	Intimacy
Stability	Ordinality	Coherence, continuity
		First order change
		Negative feedback loops
	Mind/minded	Definition of the situation, consensus, working agreement, communication
Transactions	Feedback	Closed/open
Integration		Bonds
Entropy	Disintegration	Disorganization, dysfunction

NOTES

37. Current usage of "boundary" employs the word to refer to a family's internal structure (Minuchin, 1974) and, also, to refer to the differentiation of the family from its context.

REFERENCES

Albee, E. (1962). *Who's afraid of Virginia Woolf?* New York: Atheneum.

Bateson, G. (1979). *Mind and nature.* Toronto: Bantam Books.

Bateson, G. (1972). *Steps to an ecology of mind.* New York: Ballantine.

Becvar, R. J. & Becvar, D. S. (1982). *Systems theory and family therapy.* Lanham, MD: University Press of America.

Belsky, J. (1984). The determinent of parenting: A process model. *Child Development, 55,* 83–96.

Bertalanffy, L. von. (1968). *General systems theory foundations, development, applications.* New York: Braziller.

Bogdan, J. L. (1984). Family organization as an ecology of ideas: An alternative to the reification of family systems. *Family Process, 23,* 375–388.

Bolton, C. D. (1961). Mate selection as the development of a relationship. *Mariage and Family Living, 23,* 234–240.

Boss, P. & Greenberg, J. (1984). Family boundary ambiguity: A new variable in family stress theory. *Family Process, 23,* 535–546.

Brodbeck, M. (1968). Freedom, determinism, and morality. In M. Brodbeck (Ed.), *Readings in the philosophy of the social sciences,* (pp. 669–677). New York: Macmillan, 1968.

Constantine, L. L. (1983). Dysfunction and failure in open family systems, I: Application of a unified theory. *Journal of Marriage and the Family, 45,* 725–738.

Cuber, J. C., & Harroff, P. B. (1965). *Sex and the significant Americans.* Baltimore: Penguin.

Dell, P. F. (1982). Beyond homeostasis: Toward a concept of coherence. *Family Process, 21,* 21–41.

Dell, P. F. (1985). Understanding Bateson and Maturana: Toward a biological foundation for the social sciences. *Journal of Marital and Family Therapy, 11*(1), 1–20.

Firignano, S. W. & Lachman, M. E. (1985). Permeality change during the transition to parenthood: The role of perceived infant temperment. *Developmental Psychology, 21* (3), 558–567.

Fowler, H. W. & Fowler, F. G. (1964). *The concise Oxford dictionary.* Oxford: Clarendon.

Galvin, K. M. & Brommel, B. J. (1982). *Family communication.* Glenview, IL: Scott Foresman.

Gelles, R. J. & Maynard, P. E. (1984). Applying research in family violence to a family systems approach to intervention. Paper presented at the Annual Meeting of the National Council on Family Relations, San Francisco, California.

Giles-Sims, J. (1983). *Wife battering: A systems theory approach.* New York: Guilford Press.

Haley, J. (1963). *Strategies of psychotherapy.* New York: Grune & Stratton.

Hampden-Turner, C. (1981). *Maps of the mind.* New York: Macmillan.

Henry, J. (1965). *Pathways to madness.* New York: Vintage.

Hill, R. (1958). Generic features of families under stress. *Social Casework, 39,* 139–150.

Hill, R. (1971). Modern systems theory and the family: A confrontation. *Family Sociology,* 264–283.

Hoffman, L. (1971). Deviation-amplifying processes in natural groups. In J. Haley (Ed.), *Changing families* (pp. 285–311). New York: Grune & Stratton, 1971.

Kaplan, A. (1964). *The conduct of inquiry.* San Francisco: Chandler.

Kantor, D. & Lehr, W. (1975). *Inside the family.* San Francisco: Jossey-Bass.

Klein, D. M. & Hill, R. (1979). Determinants of family problem-solving effectiveness. In W. R. Burr, R. Hill, F. I. Nye, & I. L.

Reiss (Eds.), *Contemporary theories about the family, Volume I,* (pp. 493–548). New York: The Free Press, 1979.

Koestler, A. (1978). *Janus.* New York: Random House.

Koestler, A. (1954). *The invisible writing.* New York: Macmillan.

Laing, R. D. & Esterson, A. (1964). *Sanity, madness and the family.* Harmondsworth: Penguin.

Land, G. T. & Kenneally, C. (1977). Creativity, reality, and general systems: A personal viewpoint. *Journal of Creative Behavior, 11*(1), 12–35.

Levant, R. F. (1984). *Family therapy: A comprehensive view.* Englewood Cliffs, New Jersey: Prentice-Hall, Inc.

Maturana, H. R. (1978). Biology of language: The epistemology of reality. In G. A. Miller and E. Lenneberg (Eds.), *Psychology and biology of language and thought,* (pp. 27–53). New York: Academic Press, 1978.

Maruyama, M. (1968). The second cybernetics: Deviation-amplifying mutual causal processes. In W. Buckley (Ed.), *Modern systems research for the behavioral scientist* (pp. 304–313). Chicago: Aldine, 1968.

McCubbin, H. I. & Patterson, J. M. (1983). The family stress process: The double ABCX model of adjustment and adaptation. *Marriage and Family Review, 6*(1 & 2), 7–37.

Miller, D. R. (1984). Commentary: A family is a family is a family. *Family Process, 23,* 389–395.

Minuchin, S. (1974). *Families and family therapy.* Cambridge: Harvard University Press.

Montgomery, J. (1981). *Family crisis as process.* Lanham, MD: University Press of America.

Montgomery, J. (1985). Family compromise, members' definitions and crisis-related behavior. *Canadian Home Economics Journal, 35*(2), 89–93.

Nichols, M. P. (1984). *Family therapy concepts and methods.* New York: Gardner Press.

Olson, D. H., Sprenkle, D. H., & Russell, C. S. (1979). Circumplex model of marital and family systems: I. Cohesion and adaptability dimensions, family types, and clinical applications. *Family Process, 18,* 3–28.

Olson, D. H., Russell, C. S. & Sprenkle, D. H. (1983). Circumplex model of marital and family system: VI. Theoretical update. *Family Process, 22,* 69–83.

Olson, D. H. & McCubbin, H. I. (1982). Circumplex marital and family systems V: Application to family stress and crisis intervention. In H. I. McCubbin, A. E. Cauble, & J. M. Patterson (Eds.), *Family stress, coping, and social support, (pp. 48–68). Springfield, IL: C. Thomas, 1982.*

O'Neill, N., & O'Neill, G. (1972). Open marriage. New York: Avon.

Reiss, D., & Oliveri, M. E. (1980). Family paradigm and family coping: A proposal for linking the family's intrinsic adaptive capacities to its responses to stress. *Family Relations, 29*(4), 431–444.

Reiss, D., & Oliveri, M. E. (1983). The family's construction of social reality and its ties to kin network: An explanation of causal direction. *Journal of Marriage and the Family, 45,*(1), 81–91.

Rifkin, J. (1980). *Entropy.* Toronto: Bantam.

Speer, D. C. (1970). Family systems: Morphostasis and morphogenesis, or Is homeostasis enough? *Family Process, 9,* 259–278.

Straus, M. A. (1980). A sociological perspective on the causes of family violence. In M. R. Green (Ed.), Violence and the family, (pp. 7–31). Boulder, CO: Westview Press, 1980.

Straus, M. A., Gelles, R. J. & Steinmetz, S. B. (1980). *Behind closed doors: Violence in the American family.* Garden City, NY: Anchor/ Doubleday.

Turner, R. H. (1970). *Family interaction.* New York: Wiley.

Vogel, E. V. & Bell, N. W. (1960). The emotionally disturbed child as the family scapegoat. In N. W. Bell & E. F. Vogel (Eds.), *The family,* (pp. 382–397). Glencoe: Free Press, 1960.

Walker, A. J. (1985). Reconceptualizing family stress. *Journal of Marriage and the Family, 47,* 827–837.

Watzlawick, P., Beavin, J. H., & Jackson, D. D. (1967). *Pragmatics of human communication.* New York: Norton.

Watzlawick, P., Weakland, J. H., & Fisch, R. (1974). *Change.* New York: Norton.

Wilson, E. K. (1966). *Sociology.* Homewood, IL: Dorsey.

INDEX